W9-CRS-113

ALL ABOUT® Reading

The program that takes the struggle out of reading

Level 1

by Marie Rippel

All rights reserved. No portion of this publication may be reproduced by any means, including duplicating, photocopying, electronic, mechanical, recording, the World Wide Web, e-mail, or otherwise, without written permission from the publisher.

Copyright © 2014, 2011 by All About® Learning Press, Inc.
Printed in the United States of America

All About® Learning Press, Inc.
615 Commerce Loop
Eagle River, WI 54521

ISBN 978-1-935197-24-9
v. 1.3

Editor/Contributor: Renée LaTulippe
Cover Design: Dave LaTulippe
Page Layout: Renée LaTulippe

The *All About Reading* Level 1 Teacher's Manual is part of the *All About® Reading* program.

For more books in this series, go to www.AllAboutReading.com.

Dear Parents and Teachers,

Learning to read is an exciting time in children's lives. It is also an important time because what children learn about reading at this age, and how they feel about the process, will affect their attitude toward reading for the rest of their lives.

The *All About Reading* program is unique in the world of language arts. It is a complete, phonics-based, multisensory, "open-and-go" program that focuses on all the essential components of reading. You can rest assured that your student will learn to read. In fact, we guarantee it!

Enjoy this exciting new learning adventure with your student!

Contents

3 Appendices

1
Preparing for Level 1

What Do You Need?

In addition to this Teacher's Manual, you will need the following items:

1. Student Packet

The Student Packet contains:
- *Blast Off to Reading!* activity book
- Phonogram Cards and Word Cards
- Viewfinder Bookmark

2. Interactive Kit

The Interactive Kit contains:
- Letter Tiles
- Divider Cards
- *Phonogram Sounds* app
- Reading Review Box (Deluxe Kit)
- Stickers for the Progress Chart (Deluxe Kit)
- Tote Bag (Deluxe Kit)

(If you did not get the Reading Review Box, you will need an index card box.)

3. Readers

- *Run, Bug, Run!*
- *The Runt Pig*
- *Cobweb the Cat*

4. Common Craft Materials

- Crayons, scissors, glue, tape, stapler

5. 2' x 3' Magnetic White Board

A magnetic white board is optional, but highly recommended.

6. Reading Games with Ziggy the Zebra

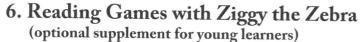

(optional supplement for young learners)

If your child enjoyed working with Ziggy in the *All About Reading* Pre-reading program, or if you are working with a child six or under, consider adding this supplement.

What You Should Know about This Program

First of all, you can do this! *All About Reading* is a scripted, open-and-go program, developed for busy parents, teachers, and tutors who want to teach reading in the most effective way possible. It doesn't require long periods of study, you don't have to develop your own lesson plans, and you don't have to stress over what to teach next. If you can follow basic instructions, you can teach reading with this method—because everything is laid out for you, step by step. You get solid grounding in how to teach reading, without being overwhelmed.

Your student will be actively involved in the learning process. This is a true multisensory program: your student will learn through sight, sound, and touch. Everything is taught in context, and your student applies new learning right away. Your student will be engaged in thinking, processing, comparing, and learning.

Students who use the *All About Reading* method tend to feel a sense of excitement in learning. And they should! They are learning how to think, explore, and grow in their abilities. They feel successful as they see continual progress.

There are no gaps in this program. Your student will be taught everything he or she needs to know about reading, so no guessing is required. Each new concept builds upon the previous one, and no steps are skipped.

There are five key components of reading—and our program teaches all of them thoroughly. Those components are:

- Phonological Awareness
- Phonics and Decoding
- Fluency
- Vocabulary
- Comprehension

Most importantly, *All About Reading* is committed to results. The *All About Reading* program has a very focused mission: to enable you to teach your student to read as quickly as you can, while guaranteeing retention and enjoyment. Our approach to reading develops students into confident readers who absorb and retain new information.

If you ever have a question as you are teaching, please feel free to contact me through our website at www.allaboutreading.com.

Prepare for Your First Lesson

Now you are ready to set up for your reading lessons! After this initial prep time, the lesson plans will be "open-and-go."

You will need:

- ☒ Set of color-coded Letter Tiles
- ☒ *Phonogram Sounds* app
- ☒ *Blast Off to Reading!* activity book
- ☒ Magnetic white board

- ☒ Two small baggies
- ☒ Divider Cards
- ☒ Reading Review Box
  or index card box

Estimated prep time: 30 minutes

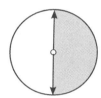

Prepare Your Letter Tiles

Take out the laminated Letter Tiles sheets. Separate the letter tiles and labels on the perforations.

Apply the magnets to the back of the letter tiles. Stick one magnet on the back of each letter tile and two magnets on the back of each label. (If you will be using the letter tiles on a tabletop instead of a magnetic white board, skip this step.)

Get two small plastic baggies. Label one bag *Level 1* and the other bag *Levels 2–4*.

Put in your *Level 1* baggie:

- two sets of letters a to z
- letter tiles th, sh, ch, ck, ng, nk, and third s
- Consonant Teams label

Put the remaining tiles and labels, including the blank ones, in the *Levels 2–4* baggie. Store the baggie in your *All About Reading* tote bag or other safe place.

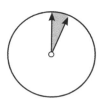

Estimated prep time:
5 minutes

Set Up Your Magnetic White Board

You'll be using the letter tiles in every lesson.

Set up your magnetic white board with one set of letter tiles <u>a</u> to <u>z</u>, as follows:

Use both the blue and the red <u>y</u> tiles in this initial setup. Store the remaining letters in your *Level 1* baggie.

As a shorthand way to represent the sounds of letters in this teacher's manual, we use slashes. For example, /m/ stands for the spoken sound *mmm* as in *monkey*.

You will also see two other sound symbols:

- A straight line above a letter, as in /ā/, represents the long vowel sound. This symbol is called a *macron*.

- A "smile" above a letter, as in /ă/, represents the short vowel sound. This symbol is called a *breve*.

For a complete list of sounds, along with key words, please see Appendix B.

What do the different colors mean?
- Blue tiles are consonants and consonant teams.
- Red tiles are vowels and vowel teams.
- Purple tiles are for the sound of /er/.
- Yellow tiles are for <u>r</u>-controlled combinations.
- Green tiles are for the sound of /sh/.
- Orange tiles are for miscellaneous symbols and letters.

You'll learn about each category when you get to it.

Why are there two <u>y</u>'s?
- <u>Y</u> can be a consonant or a vowel, depending on the word.
- When it is a consonant, it says /y/.
- When it is a vowel, it can say /ĭ/, /ī/, or /ē/.

What will happen with the other letter tiles that are left in my *Level 1* baggie?
- Starting in Lesson 16, we will gradually add the remaining letter tiles to the board.
- Keep the baggie in a safe place (such as your reading tote bag) until the tiles are needed.

What if I don't have a magnetic white board?
A magnetic white board makes it easier and faster to set up for your reading lessons, but if you don't have a magnetic white board, you can set up the letter tiles right on your table. The lesson plans are worded as if you are using a magnetic white board, but please know that you can do exactly the same thing on your tabletop.

Prepare for Your First Lesson

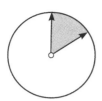

Prepare Your Reading Review Box

The Reading Review Box organizes your flashcards so review time can be productive for your student. Every lesson, except the first one, starts with review. Whether you use our custom Reading Review Box or your own index card box, follow the instructions below to set it up.

Place the divider cards in your box. The divider cards are numbered 1-6 so you can be sure to get them in the correct order.

Locate the yellow Phonogram Cards in the Student Packet. Separate the perforated cards and place them behind the yellow tabbed divider called *Phonogram Cards–Future Lessons*.

Locate the green Word Cards in the Student Packet. Separate the perforated cards and place them behind the green tabbed divider called *Word Cards–Future Lessons*.

Estimated prep time:
5 minutes

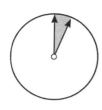

Scan the QR code below to download the *Phongram Sounds* app.

Preview the Letter Sounds

If you look ahead to the next several lessons, you will see that you'll be teaching the sounds of one to four letters at a time. You can listen to the correct pronunciation of these sounds with the *Phonogram Sounds* app. Download the app for your computer, tablet, or phone at www.allaboutlearningpress.com/phonogram-sounds-app or scan the QR code. *(Note: If you'd prefer not to download the app, a CD-ROM version is available for purchase.)*

- **Open the program and click on the letter m, which is the first letter you will be teaching in Lesson 1.** You'll hear the sound of the letter m: /m/.

- **Next, click on the letter s, which is the second letter you will be teaching.** You'll hear both sounds for the letter s: /s/–/z/. In Lesson 1, you will only be teaching the first sound, /s/. Later, in Lesson 10, you will teach the second sound. The same is true for all of the letter tiles in Level 1 that have more than one sound: first we teach the most common sound, and within a short period of time, we teach the remaining sounds.

- **If you are ever unsure about how to pronounce the sounds of the letters** at any point in the program, refer to the *Phonogram Sounds* app.

For letters with more than one sound, you may choose to teach all the sounds up front, and that is perfectly acceptable. Simply teach the multiple sounds, and then let your student know that you will be working with the first sound for the rest of the lesson. You'll work with the remaining sounds in future lessons.

The short vowel sounds are generally more difficult for students to remember, so when the vowels are taught, we add hand motions to make them more memorable. For example, the hand motion for the sound of /ă/ as in *apple* is to cup your hand as if you are holding an apple.

Preview the Lesson Layout

Turn to Lesson 3 on page 37. This is a typical lesson. Most lessons consist of these five parts:

1. **Before You Begin.** In this section, you may be prompted to preview the sounds of the letters you will be teaching, or place new letter tiles on the magnetic white board, or get a quick introduction to new terminology. This section never takes more than a couple of minutes, and then you'll be ready to call your student to the table.

2. **Review.** You'll give your student a quick review of previously-taught concepts.

3. **New Teaching.** This is the hands-on portion of the lesson. Your student will work with the letter tiles, activity sheets, and fluency exercises, and/or read from the decodable readers.

4. **Read-Aloud Time.** This is the time you spend reading to your student from a book of your choice.

5. **Track Your Progress** with the Progress Chart.

Flip through the remaining lessons. You'll see that some lessons are longer and others are shorter. Depending on the student and how much time you have allocated to the lesson, you may sometimes be able to cover more than one lesson. If your student has thoroughly understood a lesson and you sense that he is ready for the next challenge, move straight into the next lesson.

If you are working with a younger student, you may only make it through part of a lesson, especially with the longer lessons. Do what is best for your individual student. Don't feel like you must push through an entire lesson if your student isn't ready. Simply mark your place in the lesson plans and continue from that point the next day.

Remember to start every lesson with a quick review before picking up where you left off!

A common question parents ask is "How much time should I spend on reading lessons?"

There is no pat answer, since situations vary widely depending on the student's age, attention span, and previous experience.

In general, the ideal scenario is to do short lessons five days a week.

If you want to make faster progress (with an older child, for example), you might try holding two twenty-minute reading lessons per day, five days a week, plus daily read-alouds. But if you feel your student is getting "bogged down," back off to one lesson per day to let the concepts sink in.

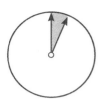

Preview the *Blast Off to Reading!* Activity Book

The *Blast Off* activity book contains
- Progress Chart
- Activity sheets
- Fluency Practice sheets
- Certificate of Completion

Note that each student should have his own activity book.

The lesson plans in this Teacher's Manual will tell you which pages you need for the lesson. You'll find that the pages in the activity book are perforated for easy removal.

The Fluency Practice sheets are the most important part of the *Blast Off* activity book. Fluency practice will help your student move from sounding out words letter by letter to instant recognition of words. The lessons include many tips and techniques for helping your student develop fluency.

Some of the matching or game sheets will appeal mainly to younger children. If you are working with an older student, feel free to skip any of the hands-on activity sheets that your student would not enjoy.

For many of the activity sheets, you will need these basic supplies:
- tape
- scissors
- stapler
- crayons or markers (optional)

Prepare for Read-Aloud Time

Toward the end of each lesson, you will be prompted to read to your student for twenty minutes. The daily read-aloud time may seem like a simple part of the reading lessons, but it's actually one of the most important components.

Here are some things to think about as you plan ahead for read-aloud time:

- **Figure out the best time of day for your read-aloud time.** You might find it easiest to connect read-aloud time to something else that you already do every day. After lunch, recess, or a specific class often works well. If you are a parent, bedtime is a natural time for enjoying books together.

- **Gather a variety of books, both fiction and non-fiction.** To keep interest high, look for books related to your student's specific interests and hobbies. You can also stimulate new interests by choosing read-alouds on topics that are completely new to your student.

- **Decide how you will minimize distractions.** At home, turn off the TV, computer, and telephone. Clear away competing toys and games. If you have a wiggly child, you can help him concentrate on the story by allowing him to play quietly while you read. Some students will be fine just holding a toy, while others might prefer to build with blocks, knead clay, or color quietly. For some children, it is easier to stay in one place and pay attention to what you are reading if they don't have to remain perfectly still.

Read-Aloud Time is so important because while your student is listening to good books, he'll also be

- gaining important background knowledge on a wide variety of subjects;
- developing a larger vocabulary; and
- hearing a variety of language patterns.

Once your student begins to read independently, his reading comprehension will be much higher because you've given him these huge benefits through daily read-aloud time.

Decide Where to Post the Progress Chart

You will find the Progress Chart on page 5 of the *Blast Off to Reading!* activity book. Remove the chart on the perforation.

Decide where to place the Progress Chart so your student can follow his own accomplishments. Choose a prominent place like a bulletin board, the refrigerator, the back of a door, or another easily accessible area.

After each lesson has been completed, have your student color in or place a sticker over the next star on the chart.

The Progress Chart is a motivating part of the lessons for many students because it is a visual reminder of the progress they have made toward reading independently.

Now You Are Ready to Teach Reading!

2

Complete Step-by-Step
Lesson Plans

Lesson 1 - Letters <u>m</u>, <u>s</u>, <u>p</u>, and <u>a</u>

This lesson will teach words containing the letters <u>m</u>, <u>s</u>, <u>p</u>, and <u>a</u>.

You will need: ☐ Phonogram Cards 1-4   ☐ Word Cards 1-3
☐ *Blast Off to Reading!* page 7   ☐ Progress Chart

Before You Begin

At the beginning of many of the lessons, you will find a "Before You Begin" section enclosed in a box. Review these instructions before you begin the lesson.

The actual lesson plan you will teach to your student begins *after* the boxed section.

Preview the Sounds of the Letters

The four letters in today's lesson were chosen because their sounds are easy for students to learn, and they can be used right away to form simple words. Listen to the *Phonogram Sounds* app for a demonstration of the phonogram sounds.

m The letter <u>m</u> says /m/ as in *moon*.

s The letter <u>s</u> makes two sounds: /s/ as in *sun* and <u>z</u> as in *has*. The first sound of <u>s</u> is covered in this lesson, and the second sound of <u>s</u> is taught in Lesson 10.

p The letter <u>p</u> says /p/ as in *pig*. Be sure that you and your student don't add /uh/ to the end of the sound, as in /puh/.

a The letter <u>a</u> has three basic sounds: /ă/–/ā/–/ah/. The first sound is considered the short sound of <u>a</u> (/ă/ as in *apple*), and that is the sound that is taught in this lesson. The remaining sounds for <u>a</u> will be taught in Lesson 44.

Short vowel sounds tend to be trickier to remember than consonant sounds. To help your student remember the sound of short <u>a</u> (/ă/), we will use a hand motion. **Tip!**

Cup your hand as if you are holding an apple. "When we say /ă/, let's pretend that we are holding an apple. Say the sound of <u>a</u> like this: /ă/–/ă/–apple." *Student pretends to hold an apple and says /ă/–/ă/–apple.*

To further cement this sound in your student's mind, take a bite out of the pretend apple with a loud crunch! The more dramatic you make this activity, the better your student will remember it.

New Teaching

Teach New Letter Sounds

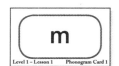

Hold up the Phonogram Card for the letter <u>m</u>.

"This letter says /m/."

"Now it's your turn. What does this letter say?" *Student says /m/.*

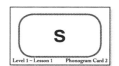

Hold up the Phonogram Card for the letter <u>s</u>.

"This letter says /s/."

"Your turn. What does this letter say?" *Student says /s/.*

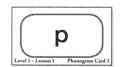

Hold up the Phonogram Card for the letter <u>p</u>.

"This letter says /p/."

"Your turn." *Student says /p/.*

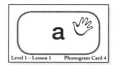

Hold up the Phonogram Card for the letter <u>a</u>.

"This letter says /ă/."

Cup your hand as if you are holding an apple. "When we say /ă/, let's pretend that we are holding an apple. Say the sound of <u>a</u> like this: /ă/–/ă/–apple." *Student pretends to hold an apple and says /ă/–/ă/–apple.*

Shuffle the cards and review them several times.

 File the flashcards behind the **Phonogram Cards Review** divider in your student's Reading Review Box. The cards will be reviewed at the beginning of the next lesson.

> **Tip!**
>
> Notice the hand on the card for <u>a</u>. This indicates that there is a hand motion that goes along with the sound. You may wish to point out this symbol to your student.
>
> Vowel sounds are usually more difficult for students to learn. We make it easier by adding hand motions and teaching only one new vowel sound at a time.

Now practice the same sounds using the letter tiles. Pull these four letter tiles down into your work space. Point to each one in random order, and ask your student to tell you the sound that each tile makes.

m s p a

Practice until your student can say the sound of each letter accurately.

New Teaching
(continued)

Demonstrate How to Blend Sounds

Build the word *map* with letter tiles.

"Watch while I show you how we sound out words."

"I touch each letter tile in order, and I say the sound of that letter."

Touch the <u>m</u> and say /*m*/.

Touch the <u>a</u> and say /*ă*/.

Be sure your student uses the <u>Tip!</u> **pointer finger of his dominant hand for this exercise.**

Touch the <u>p</u> and say /*p*/.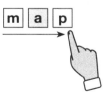

Now go back to the beginning of the word and blend the sounds together, as follows:

Slide your finger under the letters <u>m</u>-<u>a</u> and say /*mă*/.

Start at the beginning of the word again. Slide your finger under the letters <u>m</u>-<u>a</u>-<u>p</u> and say *map* slowly.

Finally, read the word *map* at a normal pace, as we do when we speak.

When your student reads the word in this <u>Tip!</u> **last step, you may need to prompt him to say the word "fast like we talk."**

Using the same procedure for blending, have your student sound out the word *Sam*.

Lesson 1: Letters <u>m</u>, <u>s</u>, <u>p</u>, and <u>a</u>

25

Play "Change the Word"

Leave the word *Sam* on the board. $\boxed{\text{s}}\,\boxed{\text{a}}\,\boxed{\text{m}}$

"I'm going to change the first letter of this word."

"What does this new word say?" Encourage your student to sound out the new word. *Pam.*

Build the word *sap*. $\boxed{\text{s}}\,\boxed{\text{a}}\,\boxed{\text{p}}$

"Sound out this word." *Student sounds out the word* sap.

Change the first letter to form the word *map*.

"What does this new word say?" *Student sounds out the word* map.

Return the letter tiles to their place in the alphabet.

Teach Vowels and Consonants

"Some of the letter tiles are red. Say the names of the letters on the red tiles." *A̲, e̲, i̲, o̲, u̲, and y̲.*

"The red tiles are *vowels*: a̲, e̲, i̲, o̲, u̲, and sometimes y̲."

"The blue tiles are *consonants*. C̲ is a consonant. P̲ is a consonant." Point to the letter tiles as you mention them.

"Can you tell me some other consonants?" *Student names some consonants.*

Point to the two y̲ tiles. $\boxed{\text{y}}\,\boxed{\text{y}}$

"The letter y̲ can be a vowel or a consonant. That's why we have a red y̲ and a blue y̲.

If you are using *Reading Games with Ziggy the Zebra*, you can play "Apples for Ziggy" to reinforce the concept of vowels and consonants.

New Teaching
(continued)

Don't Forget

If you are working with an older student, feel free to skip any of the activity sheets that your student wouldn't enjoy.

Complete Activity Sheet

Pam Sam map sap

Word Match

Remove page 7 from the *Blast Off* activity book.

Cut out the words from the bottom of the page.

Have your student paste or tape the words under the matching picture.

Explain that names start with a capital letter.

"Which of these words are names?" *Pam and Sam.*

"Which of these words rhyme?" *Pam and Sam, map and sap.*

Practice Reading Words

Have your student practice reading the words on Word Cards 1-3.

| am | Sam | map |
| Level 1 – Lesson 1 — Word Card 1 | Level 1 – Lesson 1 — Word Card 2 | Level 1 – Lesson 1 — Word Card 3 |

File the flashcards behind the **Word Cards Review** divider in your student's Reading Review Box. The cards will be reviewed at the beginning of the next lesson.

Read-Aloud Time   Read a Story or Poem

Read aloud to your student for twenty minutes.

Lesson 1: Letters <u>m</u>, <u>s</u>, <u>p</u>, and <u>a</u>

Track Your Progress

Mark the Progress Chart

After each lesson has been completed, have your student color in or place a sticker over that lesson number on the chart.

Lesson 1: Letters <u>m</u>, <u>s</u>, <u>p</u>, and <u>a</u>

Lesson 2 - Letters <u>n</u>, <u>t</u>, <u>b</u>, and <u>j</u>

This lesson will teach words containing the letters <u>n</u>, <u>t</u>, <u>b</u>, and <u>j</u>.

You will need: ☐ Phonogram Cards 5-8   ☐ Word Cards 4-12

☐ *Blast Off to Reading!* pages 9-11

Before You Begin

Preview the Sounds of the Letters

Listen to the *Phonogram Sounds* app for a demonstration of the phonogram sounds in today's lesson.

| n | The letter <u>n</u> says /n/ as in *nest*. If your student has difficulty discriminating between the sounds of /n/ and /m/, have him watch your lips as you pronounce the sounds.

| t | The letter <u>t</u> says /t/ as in *tent*. Be sure that you and your student don't add /uh/ to the end of the sound, as in /tuh/.

| b | The letter <u>b</u> says /b/ as in *bat*. It is impossible to say /b/ in isolation without any trace of /uh/ at the end, but clip the /uh/ as short as possible.

| j | The letter <u>j</u> says /j/ as in *jam*. Be sure that you and your student don't add /uh/ to the end of the sound, as in /juh/.

Look Ahead to the Review Section

You'll see that each lesson starts with a Review section. Review covers two main areas: Phonograms and Word Cards.

You'll use the Reading Review Box to keep track of what has been mastered and what still needs to be reviewed. If your student knows the Phonogram or Word Card without prompting and you feel that the card has been mastered, place the card behind the **Mastered** divider. If the card has not yet been mastered, place it behind the **Review** divider so it can be reviewed again in the next lesson.

Before You Begin
(continued)

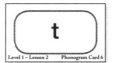

How do you know when your student has mastered a card?

If your student...
- says the pure, clipped sound without adding /uh/ at the end—for example, he says /p/, not /puh/;
- responds quickly and easily when you hold up the card; and
- does not hesitate to think of the answer

and you have no doubt that your student knows the card thoroughly...

...then that card is mastered! Move it behind the Mastered divider.

Review

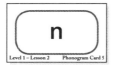

Phonogram Cards

Review the Phonogram Cards that are behind the Review divider in your student's Reading Review Box. Show the card to your student and have him say the sound. If necessary, remind your student of the sound.

Word Cards

Review the Word Cards that are behind the Review divider in your student's Reading Review Box. If your student has difficulty reading the word, build the word with letter tiles and have your student sound it out using the procedure shown in Appendix C: Full Blending Procedure.

Ask your student to point to some vowels and some consonants.

New Teaching

Teach New Letter Sounds

n

Level 1 – Lesson 2   Phonogram Card 5

Hold up the Phonogram Card for the letter n.

"This letter says /n/."

"Now it's your turn. What does this letter say?" *Student says /n/.*

t

Level 1 – Lesson 2   Phonogram Card 6

Hold up the Phonogram Card for the letter t.

"This letter says /t/."

"Your turn. What does this letter say?" *Student says /t/.*

Lesson 2: Letters n, t, b, and j

New Teaching
(continued)

If you are using *Reading Games with Ziggy the Zebra*, you can play "Ziggy at the Market" for a fun way to practice the Phonogram Cards.

Hold up the Phonogram Card for the letter <u>b</u>.

"This letter says /b/."

"Your turn." *Student says /b/.*

Hold up the Phonogram Card for the letter <u>j</u>.

"This letter says /j/."

"Your turn." *Student says /j/.*

File the Phonogram Cards behind the Review divider of the Reading Review Box.

Now practice the same sounds using the letter tiles. Pull these four letter tiles down into your work space. Point to each one in random order, and ask your student to tell you the sound that each tile makes.

Practice until your student can say the sound of each letter accurately.

Practice Commonly Confused Letters

Pull down the <u>m</u> and <u>n</u> letter tiles. Randomly dictate /m/ and /n/ to test whether your student can distinguish between the two sounds and choose the correct letter tile.

If your student has difficulty telling the difference between /m/ and /n/, have him watch your mouth as you say the sounds.

Review several times, and then add a note to the Review section of the next several lessons so you remember to practice each day.

Blend Sounds with Letter Tiles

Build the word *pan* with letter tiles.

"I'll sound out this first word, and then you'll sound out the next word."

Touch the p̲ and say /p/.

Touch the a̲ and say /ă/.

Touch the n̲ and say /n/.

Now go back to the beginning of the word and blend the sounds together, as follows:

Slide your finger under the letters p̲-a̲ and say /pă/.

Start at the beginning of the word again. Slide your finger under the letters p̲-a̲-n̲ and say *pan* slowly.

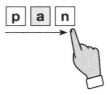

Finally, read the word *pan* at a normal pace, as we do when we speak.

Using the same procedure for blending, have your student sound out the word *nap*.

You may want to point out to your student that *pan* and *nap* contain the same letters, just in a different order.

Lesson 2: Letters n̲, t̲, b̲, and j̲

Play "Change the Word"

Leave the word *nap* on the board.

"I'm going to change the first letter of this word."

"What does this new word say?" Encourage your student to sound out the new word. *Tap.*

Continue to change one letter at a time to form the following words. Each time, have your student sound out the new word.

tap → tan → man → ban → an → at → bat → sat

Return the letter tiles to their place in the alphabet.

Complete Activity Sheets

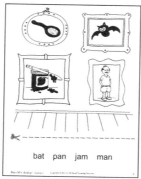

Word Match

Remove page 9 from the *Blast Off* activity book.

Cut out the words from the bottom of the page and have your student paste or tape the words under the matching picture.

Ask these questions:

"Which picture starts with the sound /j/?" *Jam.*

"Which picture starts with the sound /m/?" *Man.*

"What is the first sound in the word *bat*?" */b/.*

"What is the first sound in the word *pan*?" */p/.*

New Teaching
(continued)

Ice Cream Cones

Remove page 11 from the *Blast Off* activity book.

Cut out the ice cream scoops and cones.

Have your student read the words on each ice cream scoop. Put the rhyming words together to form ice cream desserts.

Practice Reading Words

Have your student practice reading the words on Word Cards 4-12.

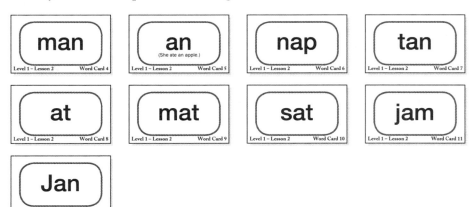

The words *an* and *Ann* are homophones (two words that sound alike but are spelled differently). A sentence has been added to the Word Card *an* and all cards containing homophones in future lessons. Your student does not read these sentences—they are there for your reference in case you wish to discuss the correct word usage.

File the Word Cards behind the Review divider of the Reading Review Box.

Lesson 2: Letters <u>n</u>, <u>t</u>, <u>b</u>, and j

Read-Aloud Time   Read a Story or Poem

Read aloud to your student for twenty minutes.

Track Your Progress

Mark the Progress Chart

Have your student mark Lesson 2 on the Progress Chart.

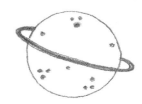

Lesson 3 - Letters g, d̲, c̲, and y̲

This lesson will teach words containing the letters g̲, d̲, c̲, and y̲, as well as the sight word the.

You will need: ☐ Phonogram Cards 9-12   ☐ Word Cards 13-21

☐ Blast Off to Reading! pages 13-17

Before You Begin

For this lesson, use the blue y̲ tile, rather than the red y̲ tile, which will be used for the vowel sounds of y̲.

Preview the Sounds of the Letters

Listen to the *Phonogram Sounds* app for a demonstration of the phonogram sounds in today's lesson.

g The letter g makes two sounds: /g/ as in *goose* and /j/ and in *gem*. The first sound of g is covered in this lesson, and the second sound of g is taught in Lesson 45.

d The letter d̲ says /d/ as in *deer*. Be sure that you and your student don't add /uh/ to the end of the sound, as in /duh/.

c The letter c̲ makes two sounds: /k/ as in *cow* and /s/ as in *city*. The first sound of c̲ is covered in this lesson, and the second sound of c̲ is taught in Lesson 44.

y The letter y̲ has four sounds: /y/–/ĭ/–/ī/–/ē/. The first sound is the consonant sound, /y/ as in *yarn*, and it is taught in this lesson. The remaining vowel sounds of y̲ are taught in Lesson 46.

Review

Review the Phonogram Cards that are behind the Review divider in your student's Reading Review Box. Show the card to your student and have him say the sound. If necessary, remind your student of the sound.

Review the Word Cards that are behind the Review divider in your student's Reading Review Box. If your student has difficulty reading the word, build the word with letter tiles and have your student sound it out using the procedure shown in Appendix C: Full Blending Procedure.

New Teaching

Teach New Letter Sounds

Teach the Phonogram Cards for the letters g, d, c, and y.

 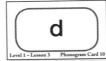 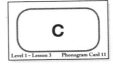 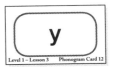

1. Hold up the Phonogram Card and say the sound.
2. Have your student repeat the sound.
3. Do a mixed review of the new Phonogram Cards.

File the Phonogram Cards behind the Review divider of the Reading Review Box.

Now practice the same sounds using the letter tiles. Pull these four letter tiles down into your work space. Point to each one in random order, and ask your student to tell you the sound that each tile makes.

| g | d | c | blue | y |

Practice until your student can say the sound of each letter accurately.

Practice Commonly Confused Letters

> **Tip!**
> Does your student confuse the letters b and d? See Appendix D for a multisensory solution.

Pull down the b and d letter tiles. Randomly dictate /b/ and /d/ to test whether your student can distinguish between the two sounds and choose the correct letter tile.

| b | d |

Next, pull down the b and p letter tiles. Randomly dictate /b/ and /p/ to see if your student can distinguish between the two sounds and choose the correct letter tile.

| b | p |

If your student has difficulty with either pair of letters, have him watch your mouth as you say the sounds. Review several times, and then add a note to the Review section of the next several lessons so you remember to practice each day.

Lesson 3: Letters g, d, c, and y

Blend Sounds with Letter Tiles

Build the word *cab* with letter tiles.

"I'll sound out this first word, and then you'll sound out the next word."

Touch the <u>c</u> and say /k/.

Touch the <u>a</u> and say /ă/.

Touch the <u>b</u> and say /b/.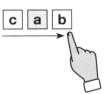

Now go back to the beginning of the word and blend the sounds together, as follows:

Slide your finger under the letters <u>c</u>-<u>a</u> and say /kă/.

Start at the beginning of the word again. Slide your finger under the letters <u>c</u>-<u>a</u>-<u>b</u> and say *cab* slowly.

Finally, read the word *cab* at a normal pace, as we do when we speak.

Using the same procedure for blending, have your student sound out the word *mad*.

m a d

> Starting over at the beginning of the word is optional. Some students need the extra support provided by this step, while others do not.
>
> Whenever you feel that your student is ready, blend all three letters without this additional step.

New Teaching
(continued)

Play "Change the Word"

Leave the word *mad* on the board.

"I'm going to change the first letter of this word."

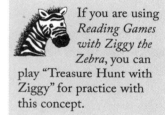

"What does this new word say?" Encourage your student to sound out the new word. *Sad.*

Continue to change one letter at a time to form the following words. Each time, have your student sound out the new word.

> **sad → pad → pan → can → cap → gap → gas**

Return the letter tiles to their place in the alphabet.

Teach that Every Word Has a Vowel

If you are using *Reading Games with Ziggy the Zebra*, you can play "Treasure Hunt with Ziggy" for practice with this concept.

"Did you notice that every word we made had a red tile—a vowel?"

Build some words from the previous activity to demonstrate this concept.

> Later, when multisyllable words are taught, your student will learn that also every syllable has at least one vowel.

Lesson 3: Letters g, d, c, and y

New Teaching
(continued)

Complete Activity Sheets

Feed the Monster
Remove page 13 from the *Blast Off* activity book.

Your student can color the monster, if desired. Make a slit in the monster's mouth and cut out the bones.

Have your student read the words on the back of the bones. After reading a word correctly, he should feed the hungry monster by sticking the bone in the monster's mouth.

Word Match
Remove page 15 from the *Blast Off* activity book.

Cut out the words from the bottom of the page. Have your student paste or tape the words under the matching picture.

Ask these questions:

"Which picture ends with the sound /g/?" *Bag.*

"Which picture ends with the sound /d/?" *Sad.*

"What is the last sound in the word *gas*?" */s/.*

"What is the last sound in the word *cap*?" */p/.*

New Teaching
(continued)

You may need to explain that a yam is a vegetable that tastes like a sweet potato. It grows underground like a regular potato, and it is orange inside.

Practice Reading Words

Have your student practice reading the words on Word Cards 13-20.

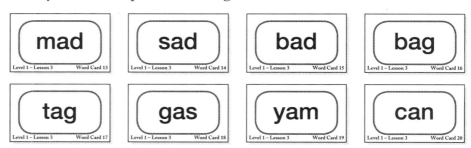

File the Word Cards behind the Review divider of the Reading Review Box.

Teach a Sight Word: *the*

Show Word Card 21 to your student.

You may wish to explain that we usually pronounce this word as /thŭ/. Sometimes we do say /thē/, but for the purposes of the flashcard review, say the more common pronunciation: /thŭ/.

"Most words follow the rules and say the sounds that we expect them to say. But there are a few words that do not. Here is one of those words."

"This word is *the*, as in *She has the balloons.*"

Point to the Bad Guy on the Word Card. "See this Bad Guy? This means that the word can't be sounded out. This is a word that you just need to remember."

Review this word several times today and then file it behind the Review divider.

Lesson 3: Letters g, d, c, and y

New Teaching
(continued)

Practice Fluency

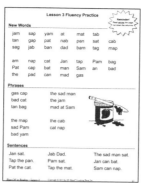

Fluency is the ability to read smoothly, accurately, and with expression.

Remove page 17 from the *Blast Off* activity book.

Have your student read from the Fluency Practice sheet.

The sentences on this activity sheet end with a period. Explain that a period is a punctuation mark used to end a sentence.

Don't Forget

Remember that this is hard work for most beginning readers, especially if they are still at the stage of sounding out each word. Reward effort with words of praise!

Tips for Using the Fluency Practice Sheets

Tip!

Over time, the Fluency Practice will help your student move from sounding out words letter by letter to instant recognition of words. This change usually happens gradually, so don't expect perfection at first.

Here are some tips to help you get the most benefit out of the Fluency Practice sheets:

1. **Place the sheet directly in front of your student.**

2. **Read across the page from left to right** to reinforce proper eye movements. Don't read down the columns.

3. **The viewfinder bookmark can help your student focus on individual words.** Either run the top edge of the bookmark under the line of text, or center the word or phrase in the cutout area.

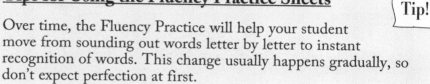

4. **Stop before your student fatigues.** You might not complete the fluency practice all in one day, depending on your student's age and attention span.

5. **Would your student benefit from reviewing the Fluency Practice sheet several times?** If so, repeat the exercise several days in a row.

6. **On the other hand, don't overwhelm your beginning reader with *too* much practice with the Fluency Practice sheets.** It is important to find the right balance for your individual student. Some students desperately need the practice provided, while others (especially younger children) are better served by reading every other line, or every third line.

Read-Aloud Time   Read a Story or Poem

Read aloud to your student for twenty minutes.

Track Your Progress

Mark the Progress Chart

Have your student mark Lesson 3 on the Progress Chart.

Lesson 3: Letters g, <u>d</u>, <u>c</u>, and <u>y</u>

Lesson 4 - Letters <u>h</u>, <u>k</u>, and <u>r</u>

This lesson will teach words containing the letters <u>h</u>, <u>k</u>, and <u>r</u>, as well as the sight word <u>a</u>.

You will need: ☐ Phonogram Cards 13-15 ☐ Word Cards 22-29
☐ *Blast Off to Reading!* pages 19-23

Before You Begin

Preview the Sounds of the Letters

Listen to the *Phonogram Sounds* app for a demonstration of the phonogram sounds in today's lesson.

| h | The letter <u>h</u> says /h/ as in *hat*.

| k | The letter <u>k</u> says /k/ as in *kite*.

| r | The letter <u>r</u> says /r/ as in *rake*. If the sound /r/ is difficult for your student to say in isolation, try having him make a growling noise like a dog: /grrr/. Then say the sound without the initial /g/ sound, leaving just the /rrr/ sound. A common mistake is to pronounce <u>r</u> as /ruh/.

Review

Review takes only a few minutes a day, yet it is critical to your student's success.

Don't skip it!

 If you are using *Reading Games with Ziggy the Zebra*, you can play "Ziggy Teaches School" whenever your student needs more practice with blending.

Phonogram Cards

Review the Phonogram Cards that are behind the Review divider in your student's Reading Review Box. Show the card to your student and have him say the sound. If necessary, remind your student of the sound.

Word Cards

Review the Word Cards that are behind the Review divider in your student's Reading Review Box. If your student has difficulty reading the word, build the word with letter tiles and have your student sound it out using the procedure shown in Appendix C: Full Blending Procedure.

Ask your student to point to some vowels and some consonants.

Review the fact that every word has at least one vowel.

New Teaching

Teach New Letter Sounds

Teach the Phonogram Cards for the letters <u>h</u>, <u>k</u>, and <u>r</u>.

1. Hold up the Phonogram Card and say the sound.
2. Have your student repeat the sound.
3. Do a mixed review of the new Phonogram Cards.

File the Phonogram Cards behind the Review divider of the Reading Review Box.

Now practice the same sounds using the letter tiles. Pull these three letter tiles down into your work space. Point to each one in random order, and ask your student to tell you the sound that each tile makes.

| h | k | r |

Practice until your student can say the sound of each letter accurately.

Blend Sounds with Letter Tiles

Build the word *rat* with letter tiles. | r | a | t |

"I'll sound out this first word, and then you'll sound out the next word."

Touch the <u>r</u> and say */r/*.

Touch the <u>a</u> and say */ă/*.

Touch the <u>t</u> and say */t/*.

Lesson 4: Letters <u>h</u>, <u>k</u>, and <u>r</u>

New Teaching
(continued)

Now go back to the beginning of the word and blend the sounds together, as follows:

Slide your finger under the letters r-a and say /ră/.

Start at the beginning of the word again. Slide your finger under the letters r-a-t and say *rat* slowly.

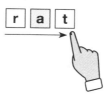

Finally, read the word *rat* at a normal pace, as we do when we speak.

Using the same procedure for blending, have your student sound out the word *had*.

h a d

Play "Change the Word"

Leave the word on the board. h a d

"I'm going to change the last letter of this word."

"What does this new word say?" Encourage your student to sound out the new word. *Ham.*

Continue to change one letter at a time to form the following words. Each time, have your student sound out the new word.

ham → hat → rat → mat → mad → had

Return the letter tiles to their place in the alphabet.

New Teaching
(continued)

Complete Activity Sheets

Letter Sounds Bingo
Remove page 19 from the *Blast Off* activity book.

Give your student something fun to use for markers, like raisins, M&Ms, coins, dried beans, or Cheerios.

Randomly call out the sounds of the letters. When a sound is called, your student should put a marker over the corresponding letter. When the student gets three in a row, he says "Bingo!"

For a longer game, have the student fill the card completely before calling bingo.

Word Match
Remove page 21 from the *Blast Off* activity book.

If necessary, explain that a yak is a large animal with very long, thick hair and horns.

Cut out the words from the bottom of the page. Have your student paste or tape the words under the matching picture.

Ask these questions:

"Which picture starts with the sound /y/?" *Yak.*

"Which two pictures end with the sound /t/?" *Rat and hat.*

"What is the last sound in the word *ham*?" /m/.

New Teaching
(continued)

Practice Reading Words

Have your student practice reading the words on Word Cards 22-28.

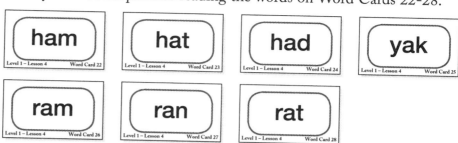

File the Word Cards behind the Review divider of the Reading Review Box.

Teach a Sight Word: *a*

Show Word Card 29 to your student.

You may wish to explain that we usually pronounce this word as /uh/. Sometimes we do say /ā/, but for the purpose of flashcard review, say the more common pronunciation: /uh/.

"Most words follow the rules and say the sounds that we expect them to say. But there are a few words that do not. Here is one of those words."

"This word is *a*, as in *I have a dog*." Pronounce *a* as /uh/, which is the most common pronunciation of this short word.

Review this word several times today and then file it behind the Review divider.

Lesson 4: Letters <u>h</u>, <u>k</u>, and <u>r</u>

New Teaching
(continued)

Don't Forget

Your beginning student isn't expected to read through the entire Fluency Practice sheet in one sitting.

Most students will still be at the stage of sounding out many of the words, and that can be tiring mental work. Stop before your student fatigues. You can always continue tomorrow.

Practice Fluency

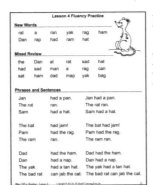

Remove page 23 from the *Blast Off* activity book.

Have your student read from the Fluency Practice sheet.

Phrases and Sentences

Beginning with this lesson, every Fluency Practice Sheet will have a section called "Phrases and Sentences." First there are two short phrases, such as *Jan* and *had a pan*. Then the phrases are combined into a sentence: *Jan had a pan*. This type of practice is called phrased reading, and it improves your student's phrasing. Phrasing is important for fluency; fluent readers are able to phrase, or break text into meaningful parts.

If your student does not need practice with phrasing, feel free to skip the first two shorter phrases and have your student read just the full sentence.

Exclamation Points

Some of the sentences on the Fluency Practice sheet contain exclamation points. Explain that exclamation points are used to show emotion or excitement. Model for your student how to read a sentence with an exclamation point. Exclamation points are used in the story your student will read in the next lesson.

Lesson 4: Letters <u>h</u>, <u>k</u>, and <u>r</u>

Read-Aloud Time   Read a Story or Poem

Read aloud to your student for twenty minutes.

Track Your Progress

Mark the Progress Chart

Have your student mark Lesson 4 on the Progress Chart.

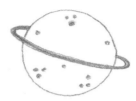

Lesson 5 - Read "Jam" and "The Tan Hat"

In this lesson, your student will apply what he has learned by reading two stories.

You will need: ☐ *Run, Bug, Run!* book

Review

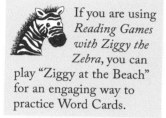 If you are using *Reading Games with Ziggy the Zebra*, you can play "Ziggy at the Beach" for an engaging way to practice Word Cards.

 Phonogram Cards

Review the Phonogram Cards that are behind the Review divider in your student's Reading Review Box. Show the card to your student and have him say the sound. If necessary, remind your student of the sound.

 Word Cards

Review the Word Cards that are behind the Review divider in your student's Reading Review Box. If your student has difficulty reading the word, build the word with letter tiles and have your student sound it out using the procedure shown in Appendix C: Full Blending Procedure.

New Teaching

Read "Jam"

"Have you ever had a friend over for dinner?" Discuss what your student and his friend ate or what they did together.

"Have you ever seen a little child get really excited about a food—like ice cream—and that is all she wants to eat?"

"The story you are about to read is about two friends who are having dinner together. Turn to page 9."

Have your student read the story "Jam."

Point Out *The End*

When your student gets to the last page of the story, read the phrase *The End*, if your student doesn't already know it. Children generally catch on to this quickly because the phrase is at a predictable part of the story—the end!

Read "The Tan Hat"

"Have you ever seen a cat play with a string or a piece of yarn? They love to bat at things, don't they?"

"Let's see what the cat in this story does. Turn to page 19."

Have your student read the story "The Tan Hat."

Read-Aloud Time

Read a Story or Poem

Read aloud to your student for twenty minutes.

Track Your Progress

Mark the Progress Chart

Have your student mark Lesson 5 on the Progress Chart.

Lesson 6 - Letters <u>i</u>, <u>v</u>, <u>f</u>, and <u>z</u>

This lesson will teach words containing the letters <u>i</u>, <u>v</u>, <u>f</u>, and <u>z</u>.

You will need: ☐ Phonogram Cards 16-19   ☐ Word Cards 30-43
☐ Blast Off to Reading! pages 25-32

Before You Begin

Preview the Sounds of the Letters

Listen to the *Phonogram Sounds* app for a demonstration of the phonogram sounds in today's lesson.

| i | The letter <u>i</u> has three basic sounds: /ĭ/–/ī/–/ē/. The first sound is considered the short sound of <u>i</u> (/ĭ/ as in *itchy*), and that is the sound that is taught in this lesson. The remaining sounds for <u>i</u> will be taught in Lesson 44.

To help your student remember the sound of short <u>i</u> (/ĭ/), we will use the following hand motion. **Tip!**

Scratch your forearm with your fingertips as if you are itchy. "When we say /ĭ/, let's pretend that we are itchy. Say the sound of <u>i</u> like this: /ĭ/–/ĭ/–itchy." *Student pretends to have an itch and says /ĭ/–/ĭ/–itchy.*

| v | The letter <u>v</u> says /v/ as in *vase*. Be sure that you and your student don't add /uh/ to the end of the sound, as in /vuh/.

| f | The letter <u>f</u> says /f/ as in *fish*.

| z | The letter <u>z</u> says /z/ as in *zipper*.

Review

Review the Phonogram Cards that are behind the Review divider in your student's Reading Review Box. Show the card to your student and have him say the sound. If necessary, remind your student of the sound.

Review the Word Cards that are behind the Review divider in your student's Reading Review Box. If your student has difficulty reading the word, build the word with letter tiles and have your student sound it out using the procedure shown in Appendix C: Full Blending Procedure.

Ask your student to point to some vowels and some consonants. (If you think your student needs further work with this concept, add this review to future lessons.)

New Teaching

Teach New Letter Sounds

Hold up the Phonogram Card for the letter i.

"This letter says / ĭ /."

Scratch your forearm with your fingertips as if you are itchy. "When we say / ĭ /, let's pretend that we are itchy. Say the sound of i like this: / ĭ /–/ ĭ /–itchy." *Student pretends to have an itch and says / ĭ /–/ ĭ /–itchy.*

Teach the Phonogram Cards for the letters v, f, and z.

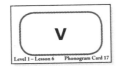 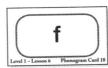 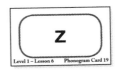

1. Hold up the Phonogram Card and say the sound.
2. Have your student repeat the sound.
3. Do a mixed review of the new Phonogram Cards.

File the Phonogram Cards behind the Review divider of the Reading Review Box.

Now practice the same sounds using the letter tiles. Pull these four letter tiles down into your work space. Point to each one in random order, and ask your student to tell you the sound that each tile makes.

Practice until your student can say the sound of each letter accurately.

Lesson 6: Letters i, v, f, and z

Blend Sounds with Letter Tiles

Build the word *dip* with letter tiles.

"I'll sound out this first word, and then you'll sound out the next word."

Touch the d̲ and say /d/.

Touch the i̲ and say /ĭ/.

Touch the p̲ and say /p/.

Now go back to the beginning of the word and blend the sounds together, as follows:

Slide your finger under the letters d̲-i̲ and say /dĭ/.

Don't Forget

Starting over at the beginning of the word is optional. Some students need the extra support provided by this step, while others do not.

Whenever you feel that your student is ready, blend all three letters without this additional step.

Start at the beginning of the word again. Slide your finger under the letters d̲-i̲-p̲ and say *dip* slowly.

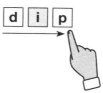

Finally, read the word *dip* at a normal pace, as we do when we speak.

Using the same procedure for blending, have your student sound out the word *fan*.

| f | a | n |

Play "Change the Word"

Build the word *him*.   h i m

"What is this word?" *Him.*

"I'm going to change the last letter of this word."

"What does this new word say?" Encourage your student to sound out the new word. *Hit.*

Continue to change one letter at a time to form the following words. Each time, have your student sound out the new word.

hit → sit → pit → bit → fit → fig →

big → bid → did → hid → rid → rip

Return the letter tiles to their place in the alphabet.

Lesson 6: Letters i, v, f, and z

New Teaching
(continued)

| Word Flippers are used in several lessons and are a fun way to practice fluency. |

If the vowels cause difficulty, have your student point  **Tip!** to the vowel and say the sound of the vowel before starting to sound out the word. For example, with the word *bit*, your student would point to the vowel and say /ĭ/ and then sound out the word from the beginning.

Use this tip whenever your student has difficulty with vowels.

Complete Activity Sheet

Word Flipper

Remove pages 25-30 from the *Blast Off* activity book.

The pages are numbered 1–3. Stack them in order, and then fold the stack in half so the word *bit* appears on top.

Staple along the folded edge. Follow the dotted lines on the first page to cut through all layers.

Have your student flip through the book randomly, reading both the real and the nonsense words that are formed.

Before starting this activity, explain to your student that some of the words are real words that they will recognize and others are nonsense words.

Reading nonsense words is a valuable activity. Think of the word *fantastic*. This word is made up of three syllables; the middle syllable by itself would read like a nonsense word. Learning to read these nonsense words will help your student read longer words later.

Practice Reading Words

Have your student practice reading the words on Word Cards 30-43.

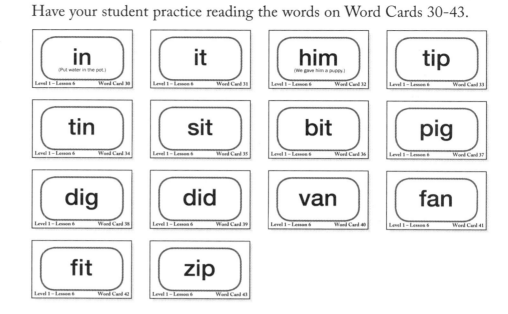

File the Word Cards behind the Review divider of the Reading Review Box.

New Teaching
(continued)

Don't Forget

Today's Fluency Practice sheet is two pages long, and you'll need to be the judge of whether your student needs all of this practice.

For older learners needing remedial work, this extra practice is critical to their success. For younger learners whose eye muscles are still developing, you should choose a reasonable number of lines to practice. Every situation is different, and you need to do what is best for your student.

Practice Fluency

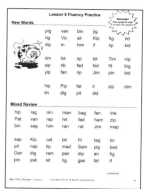

Remove pages 31-32 from the *Blast Off* activity book.

Have your student read from the Fluency Practice sheets.

Question Marks and Commas

Tip!

Some of the sentences on the Fluency Practice sheets contain question marks and commas. Explain that question marks are used to ask a question, like *How are you?* Commas are used to indicate a short pause. Don't pause as long for a comma as you do for a period.

Model for your student how to read sentences with question marks and commas.

Question marks and commas are used in the stories your student will read in the next lesson.

Read-Aloud Time
Read a Story or Poem

Read aloud to your student for twenty minutes.

Track Your Progress
Mark the Progress Chart

Have your student mark Lesson 6 on the Progress Chart.

Lesson 6: Letters <u>i</u>, <u>v</u>, <u>f</u>, and <u>z</u>

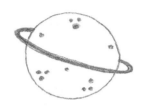

Lesson 7 - Read "Hit the Gas" and "The Bad Rat"

In this lesson, your student will apply what he has learned by reading two stories.

You will need: ☐ *Run, Bug, Run!* book

Review

 Shuffle and review the cards behind the Review dividers daily. Doing so gives your student practice with a variety of concepts presented in random order.

Review the Phonogram Cards that are behind the Review divider in your student's Reading Review Box. Show the card to your student and have him say the sound. If necessary, remind your student of the sound.

Review the Word Cards that are behind the Review divider in your student's Reading Review Box. If your student has difficulty reading the word, build the word with letter tiles and have your student sound it out using the procedure shown in Appendix C: Full Blending Procedure.

New Teaching

Read "Hit the Gas"

"Have you ever gone on a trip in a car?" Discuss where your student went or what he saw on the trip.

"In this story, a girl goes on a trip with a lot of unusual friends. Turn to page 27."

Have your student read the story "Hit the Gas."

Read "The Bad Rat"

"Have you ever been to a farm? Sometimes mice or rats live in the barns and cause trouble. They get into things and make a mess."

"Let's see what the bad rat in this story does. Turn to page 37."

Have your student read the story "The Bad Rat."

Read-Aloud Time   Read a Story or Poem

Read aloud to your student for twenty minutes.

Track Your Progress

Mark the Progress Chart

Have your student mark Lesson 7 on the Progress Chart.

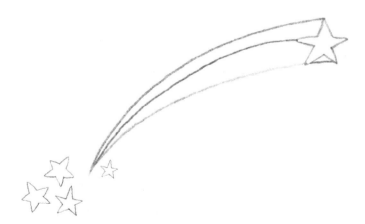

Lesson 8 - Letters <u>o</u>, <u>l</u>, and <u>w</u>

This lesson will teach words containing the letters <u>o</u>, <u>l</u>, and <u>w</u>, as well as the sight word <u>of</u>.

You will need: ☐ Phonogram Cards 20-22   ☐ Word Cards 44-54

☐ *Blast Off to Reading!* pages 33-36

Before You Begin

Preview the Sounds of the Letters

Listen to the *Phonogram Sounds* app for a demonstration of the phonogram sounds in today's lesson.

o   The letter <u>o</u> has four basic sounds: /ŏ/–/ō/–/o͞o/–/ŭ/. The first sound is considered the short sound of <u>o</u> (/ŏ/ as in *otter*), and that is the sound that is taught in this lesson. The remaining sounds for <u>o</u> will be taught in Lesson 45.

To help your student remember the sound of short <u>o</u> (/ŏ/), we will use the following hand motion.

Tip!

Form an "o" shape with one hand and hold it to your nose. "When we say /ŏ/, let's pretend that we have a nose like an otter. Say the sound of <u>o</u> like this: /ŏ/–/ŏ/–otter." *Student makes an otter nose and says /ŏ/–/ŏ/–otter.*

l   The letter <u>l</u> says /l/ as in *leaf*. Be sure that you and your student don't add /uh/ to the end of the sound, as in /luh/.

w   The letter <u>w</u> says /w/ as in *wave*. It is impossible to say /w/ in isolation without any trace of /uh/ at the end, but clip the /uh/ as short as possible.

Review

Review the Phonogram Cards that are behind the Review divider in your student's Reading Review Box. Show the card to your student and have him say the sound. If necessary, remind your student of the sound.

Review the Word Cards that are behind the Review divider in your student's Reading Review Box. If your student has difficulty reading the word, build the word with letter tiles and have your student sound it out using the procedure shown in Appendix C: Full Blending Procedure.

New Teaching

Teach New Letter Sounds

Hold up the Phonogram Card for the letter o.

"This letter says /ŏ/."

Form an "o" shape with one hand and hold it to your nose. "When we say /ŏ/, let's pretend that we have a nose like an otter. Say the sound of o like this: /ŏ/–/ŏ/–otter." *Student makes an otter nose and says /ŏ/–/ŏ/–otter.*

Teach the Phonogram Cards for the letters l and w.

 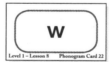

1. Hold up the Phonogram Card and say the sound.
2. Have your student repeat the sound.
3. Do a mixed review of the new Phonogram Cards.

File the Phonogram Cards behind the Review divider of the Reading Review Box.

Now practice the same sounds using the letter tiles. Pull these three letter tiles down into your work space. Point to each one in random order, and ask your student to tell you the sound that each tile makes.

Practice until your student can say the sound of each letter accurately.

New Teaching
(continued)

Blend Sounds with Letter Tiles

Build the word *lid* with letter tiles.

"I'll sound out this first word, and then you'll sound out the next word."

Touch the <u>l</u> and say /l/.

Touch the <u>i</u> and say /ĭ/.

Touch the <u>d</u> and say /d/.

Now go back to the beginning of the word and blend the sounds together, as follows:

Slide your finger under the letters <u>l</u>-<u>i</u> and say /lĭ/.

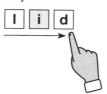

This is the last lesson in which we start at the beginning of the word for a second time. If you feel that your student still needs this step, feel free to add it in.

Start at the beginning of the word again. Slide your finger under the letters <u>l</u>-<u>i</u>-<u>d</u> and say *lid* slowly.

Finally, read the word *lid* at a normal pace, as we do when we speak.

Using the same procedure for blending, have your student sound out the word *wig*.

w i g

Play "Change the Word"

Build the word *sob*.

"What is this word?" *Sob*.

"I'm going to change the first letter of this word."

"What does this new word say?" Encourage your student to sound out the new word. *Mob*.

Continue to change one letter at a time to form the following words. Each time, have your student sound out the new word.

mob → mom → mop → top → hop → hot →

rot → pot → got

Return the letter tiles to their place in the alphabet.

Complete Activity Sheet

Word Match

Remove page 33 from the *Blast Off* activity book.

Cut out the words from the bottom of the page. Have your student paste or tape the words under the matching picture.

Ask these questions:

"Which word starts with the sound /m/?" *Mop*.

"Which two words end with the sound /g/?" *Dog and log*.

New Teaching
(continued)

Don't Forget

Remember: if the vowels cause difficulty, have your student point to the vowel and say its sound before beginning to sound out the word. For example, with the word *lap*, your student would point to the vowel and say /ă/, and then sound out the word from the beginning.

Practice Reading Words

Have your student practice reading the words on Word Cards 44-53.

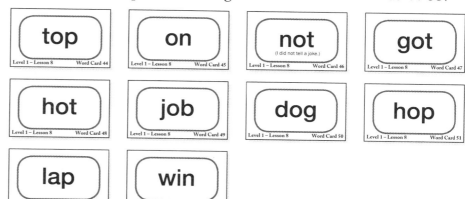

File the Word Cards behind the Review divider of the Reading Review Box.

Teach a Sight Word: *of*

Tip!

The word *of* is the only word in which the letter f says /v/.

Show Word Card 54 to your student.

"Most words follow the rules and say the sounds that we expect them to say. But there are a few words that do not. Here is one of those words."

"This word is *of*, as in *Let's get more of those fish*."

Review this word several times today and then file it behind the Review divider.

Practice Fluency

Remove pages 35-36 from the *Blast Off* activity book.

Have your student read from the Fluency Practice sheets.

Quotation Marks and Ellipses

Today's Fluency Practice sheets contain sentences with quotation marks. Point them out to your student. Explain that quotation marks are used at the beginning and end of a sentence to show that someone is speaking.

A couple of sentences on the activity sheets contain ellipses, which are a series of three dots (...) that indicate a pause in speech or an unfinished thought. Ellipses can be used in the middle or at the end of a sentence.

Model for your student how to read sentences with quotation marks and ellipses. Learning about these punctuation marks will prepare your student for the two stories he will read in the next lesson.

How Much Time?

How much time should you spend on the Fluency exercises? Only you can be the judge of that, since the answer is different for every student. For some students, there is more practice here than they need. Other students may benefit from rereading the sheets multiple times over a period of a week.

The goal in Level 1 is to keep making progress, not to achieve perfection.

Read-Aloud Time   Read a Story or Poem

Read aloud to your student for twenty minutes.

Track Your Progress   Mark the Progress Chart

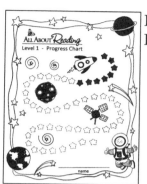

Have your student mark Lesson 8 on the Progress Chart.

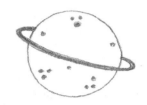

Lesson 9 - Read "The Hot Rod" and "Jan Did It"

In this lesson, your student will apply what he has learned by reading two stories.

You will need: ☐ *Run, Bug, Run!* book

Review

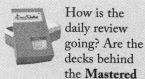

How is the daily review going? Are the decks behind the **Mastered** dividers getting bigger?

Mastered cards will be reviewed in Step 11 to keep them fresh in your student's mind.

Review the Phonogram Cards that are behind the Review divider in your student's Reading Review Box. Show the card to your student and have him say the sound. If necessary, remind your student of the sound.

Review the Word Cards that are behind the Review divider in your student's Reading Review Box. If your student has difficulty reading the word, build the word with letter tiles and have your student sound it out using the procedure shown in Appendix C: Full Blending Procedure.

New Teaching

Read "The Hot Rod"

"The story you are going to read is entitled 'The Hot Rod.' Do you know what a hot rod is? It is a fast car, or a cool car."

"Have you ever had your picture taken with a camera?" Discuss when and where your student had his picture taken.

"In the story you are about to read, someone takes a picture of a dog and makes him famous! Turn to page 47."

Have your student read the story "The Hot Rod."

New Teaching
(continued)

Read "Jan Did It"

"Do you have chores to do at home, like drying the dishes or picking up your room?" Discuss the child's chores.

"The girl in this story is very busy. Let's see what she has on her list of things to do. Turn to page 59."

On the first page of the story, make sure your student understands all the different jobs that Jan has. Check to ensure that your student understands the words *jog* (slow run), *jig* (dance), and *sob* (cry).

Have your student read the story "Jan Did It."

Read-Aloud Time

Read a Story or Poem

Read aloud to your student for twenty minutes.

Track Your Progress

Mark the Progress Chart

Have your student mark Lesson 9 on the Progress Chart.

Lesson 10 - Letter <u>u</u> and the Second Sound of <u>s</u>

This lesson will teach words containing the letter <u>u</u> and the second sound of <u>s</u>.

You will need: ☐ Phonogram Cards 2 and 23   ☐ Word Cards 55-64

☐ Blast Off to Reading! pages 37-41

Before You Begin

Preview the Sounds of the Letters

Listen to the *Phonogram Sounds* app for a demonstration of the phonogram sounds in today's lesson.

u The letter <u>u</u> has three basic sounds: /ŭ/–/ū/–/o͞o/. The first sound is considered the short sound of <u>u</u> (/ŭ/ as in *udder*), and that is the sound that is taught in this lesson. The remaining sounds for <u>u</u> will be taught in Lesson 46.

To help your student remember the sound of short <u>u</u> (/ŭ/), we will use the following hand motion.

Using both hands, do a hand motion like you are milking a cow. "When we say /ŭ/, let's pretend that we are farmers milking a cow. Say the sound of <u>u</u> like this: /ŭ/–/ŭ/–udder." *Student pretends to milk a cow and says /ŭ/–/ŭ/–udder.*

s Your student has already learned that <u>s</u> says /s/. In this lesson, we will add the second sound of s: /z/ as in *has*.

Review

Review the Phonogram Cards that are behind the Review divider in your student's Reading Review Box. Show the card to your student and have him say the sound. If necessary, remind your student of the sound.

Review the Word Cards that are behind the Review divider in your student's Reading Review Box. If your student has difficulty reading the word, build the word with letter tiles and have your student sound it out using the procedure shown in Appendix C: Full Blending Procedure.

New Teaching

Whenever you introduce a new Phonogram Card, remember to file it behind the appropriate **Review** divider in your student's Reading Review Box.

Even if your student appears to remember the new phonogram during his first introduction to it, you'll want to revisit it during your next lesson. You want to make sure that the Phonogram Card has really been mastered before moving it behind the **Mastered** divider.

Teach New Letter Sounds

Level 1 – Lesson 10   Phonogram Card 23

Hold up the Phonogram Card for the letter u.

"This letter says /ŭ/."

Using both hands, do a hand motion like you are milking a cow. "When we say /ŭ/, let's pretend that we are farmers milking a cow. Say the sound of u like this: /ŭ/–/ŭ/–udder." *Student pretends to milk a cow and says /ŭ/–/ŭ/–udder.*

Level 1 – Lesson 1   Phonogram Card 2

Take out Phonogram Card 2 and show it to your student.

"You already know that the letter s says /s/. But it also makes another sound: /z/. So the letter s makes two sounds: /s/ and /z/. Repeat after me: /s/–/z/." *Student repeats.*

File the Phonogram Cards behind the Review divider of the Reading Review Box.

Build the words *is* and *us* with letter tiles. | i | s | | u | s |

"When the letter s is at the end of a word, sometimes it says its first sound and sometimes it says its second sound. Try the first sound, and if that doesn't sound like a real word, try the second sound."

Practice this concept with the words *is* and *us*.

New Teaching
(continued)

Blend Sounds with Letter Tiles

Build the word *hut* with letter tiles. h u t

"I'll sound out this first word, and then you'll sound out the next word."

Touch the <u>h</u> and say */h/*.

Touch the <u>u</u> and say */ŭ/*.

Touch the <u>t</u> and say */t/*.

Now go back to the beginning of the word. Slide your finger under the letters <u>h</u>-<u>u</u>-<u>t</u> and say *hut* slowly.

Finally, read the word *hut* at a normal pace, as we do when we speak.

Using the same procedure for blending, have your student sound out the word *rub*. r u b

New Teaching
(continued)

Play "Change the Word"

Build the word *hum*.

"What is this word?" *Hum.*

"I'm going to change the first letter of this word."

"What does this new word say?" Encourage your student to sound out the new word. *Gum.*

Continue to change one letter at a time to form the following words. Each time, have your student sound out the new word.

gum → gun → bun → run → rub → rug →

dug → tug → bug

Return the letter tiles to their place in the alphabet.

Complete Activity Sheet

Letter Sounds Bingo

Remove page 37 from the *Blast Off* activity book.

Give your student something fun to use for markers, like raisins, M&Ms, coins, dried beans, or Cheerios.

Randomly call out the sounds of the letters. When a sound is called, your student should put a marker over the corresponding letter. When the student gets three in a row, he says "Bingo!"

For a longer game, have the student fill the card completely before calling bingo.

New Teaching
(continued)

Practice Reading Words

Have your student practice reading the words on Word Cards 55-64.

File the Word Cards behind the Review divider of the Reading Review Box.

Practice Fluency

Remove pages 39-41 from the *Blast Off* activity book.

Have your student read from the Fluency Practice sheets.

Freeing Up Mental Space for Comprehension

Tip!

Reading requires two main tasks:
1. Decoding the printed word
2. Comprehending the printed word

For the beginning reader, the decoding process is difficult and takes up much of his brain's attention. The student's mind must switch back and forth between decoding a few words and comprehending a few words.

By consistently working through the fluency exercises, your student will learn to decode the printed word more quickly and easily, freeing up more mental space for reading comprehension.

Read-Aloud Time   Read a Story or Poem

Read aloud to your student for twenty minutes.

Track Your Progress

Mark the Progress Chart

Have your student mark Lesson 10 on the Progress Chart.

Lesson 10: Letter <u>u</u> and the Second Sound of <u>s</u>

Lesson 11 - Read "Kip the Pup" and "Run, Bug, Run!"

In this lesson, your student will apply what he has learned by reading two stories.

You will need: ☐ *Run, Bug, Run!* book

Review

Review the Phonogram Cards that are behind the Review divider in your student's Reading Review Box. Show the card to your student and have him say the sound. If necessary, remind your student of the sound.

Review the Word Cards that are behind the Review divider in your student's Reading Review Box. If your student has difficulty reading the word, build the word with letter tiles and have your student sound it out using the procedure shown in Appendix C: Full Blending Procedure.

Shuffle the cards behind the **Mastered** dividers and choose a selection for review.

New Teaching

Read "Kip the Pup"

"Have you ever seen a puppy playing outside? What kinds of things do puppies like to do?" Discuss ways that puppies have fun.

"In this next story, a pup has all sorts of fun. Turn to page 69."

Have your student read the story "Kip the Pup."

Read "Run, Bug, Run!"

"In this next story, the main character is an insect. At first he is alone, but then he finds a *mob*."

"A *mob* is a *large group*."

"Say the word with me: *mob*."

"If there was a mob of mosquitoes outside last night, that means there were lots and lots of mosquitoes."

"What is the opposite of a mob?" Possible answers: *one or two, a small number.*

_____

"If you were as small as a bug, where would you hide to stay safe?" Discuss various places a small bug could hide.

"Let's see what the little bug in this story does to stay out of danger. Turn to page 79."

Have your student read the story "Run, Bug, Run!"

Read-Aloud Time

Read a Story or Poem

Read aloud to your student for twenty minutes.

Track Your Progress

Mark the Progress Chart

Have your student mark Lesson 11 on the Progress Chart.

Lesson 12 - Letter e

This lesson will teach words containing the letter e.

You will need: ☐ Phonogram Card 24   ☐ Word Cards 65-72

☐ Blast Off to Reading! pages 43-49

Before You Begin

Preview the Sounds of the Letters

Listen to the *Phonogram Sounds* app for a demonstration of the phonogram sounds in today's lesson.

e The letter e has two basic sounds: /ĕ/–/ē/. The first sound is considered the short sound of e (/ĕ/ as in *echo*), and that is the sound that is taught in this lesson. The remaining sound for e will be taught in Lesson 46.

To help your student remember the sound of short e (/ĕ/), we will use the following hand motion.

Tip!

Cup your hand to your ear as if you are listening to an echo. "When we say /ĕ/, let's pretend that we are listening to an echo. Say the sound of e like this: /ĕ/–/ĕ/–echo." *Student pretends to listen for an echo and says /ĕ/–/ĕ/–echo.*

Review

Phonogram Cards

Review the Phonogram Cards that are behind the Review divider in your student's Reading Review Box. Show the card to your student and have him say the sound. If necessary, remind your student of the sound.

Word Cards

Review the Word Cards that are behind the Review divider in your student's Reading Review Box. If your student has difficulty reading the word, build the word with letter tiles and have your student sound it out using the procedure shown in Appendix C: Full Blending Procedure.

New Teaching

Teach New Letter Sounds

Hold up the Phonogram Card for the letter <u>e</u>.

"This letter says /ĕ/."

Cup your hand to your ear as if you are listening to an echo. "When we say /ĕ/, let's pretend that we are listening to an echo. Say the sound of <u>e</u> like this: /ĕ/ –/ĕ/ –echo." *Student pretends to listen for an echo and says* /ĕ/ –/ĕ/ –echo.

File the Phonogram Card behind the Review divider of the Reading Review Box.

Pull down the new letter tile. Practice with the letter tile until your student can say the sound accurately.

e

Blend Sounds with Letter Tiles

Build the word *bed* with letter tiles. b e d

"I'll sound out this first word, and then you'll sound out the next word."

Touch the <u>b</u> and say /b/. b e d

Touch the <u>e</u> and say /ĕ/. b e d

Touch the <u>d</u> and say /d/. b e d

New Teaching
(continued)

Now go back to the beginning of the word. Slide your finger under the letters <u>b</u>-<u>e</u>-<u>d</u> and say *bed* slowly.

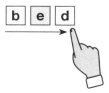

Finally, read the word *bed* at a normal pace, as we do when we speak.

Using the same procedure for blending, have your student sound out the word *set*.

Play "Change the Word"

Build the word *jet*. j e t

"What is this word?" *Jet*.

"I'm going to change the first letter of this word."

"What does this new word say?" Encourage your student to sound out the new word. *Met*.

Continue to change one letter at a time to form the following words. Each time, have your student sound out the new word.

met → men → hen → pen → pet → bet → yet → yes

Return the letter tiles to their place in the alphabet.

New Teaching
(continued)

Complete Activity Sheet

Monkeys and Bananas

Remove pages 43-46 from the *Blast Off* activity book.

Have your student choose a monkey and say the monkey's name.

The student should find the bananas that rhyme with the monkey's name and read each of the rhyming words.

The student can then choose a new monkey and repeat the exercise.

Practice Reading Words

Have your student practice reading the words on Word Cards 65-72.

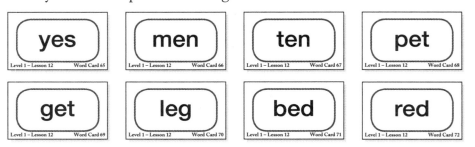

File the Word Cards behind the Review divider of the Reading Review Box.

Lesson 12: Letter <u>e</u>

New Teaching
(continued)

Practice Fluency

Remove pages 47-49 from the *Blast Off* activity book.

Have your student read from the Fluency Practice sheets.

Function Words

Tip!

Function words are short words like *the, at, an, can, am, a, if, of,* and *is.* Function words can't be described (What does *if* mean?), and they are normally unstressed (*I'kn ride'uh bike* instead of *I can ride a bike*)—yet they are the glue that holds our sentences together.

Function words make up a high percentage of our reading material, but some beginning readers need extra time to learn them. To give your student extra practice with function words, they have been sprinkled throughout the Fluency Practice sheets.

Touch the Vowel

Some students have difficulty with words containing the vowels i and e, which sound similar to untrained ears. If your student says the wrong sound, ask him to touch the vowel and say the vowel sound first. Then he should go back and sound out the word from the beginning.

Read-Aloud Time   Read a Story or Poem

Read aloud to your student for twenty minutes.

Lesson 12: Letter e

Track Your Progress

Mark the Progress Chart

Have your student mark Lesson 12 on the Progress Chart.

Lesson 13 - Read "The Gum" and "The Sad Hog"

In this lesson, your student will apply what he has learned by reading two stories.

You will need: ☐ *Run, Bug, Run!* book

Review

Review the Phonogram Cards that are behind the Review divider in your student's Reading Review Box. Show the card to your student and have him say the sound. If necessary, remind your student of the sound.

Review the Word Cards that are behind the Review divider in your student's Reading Review Box. If your student has difficulty reading the word, build the word with letter tiles and have your student sound it out using the procedure shown in Appendix C: Full Blending Procedure.

New Teaching

Read "The Gum"

"Have you ever made a big mess? How would you clean it up?" Discuss ways to clean up a mess.

"Let's see what this family does to clean up a mess. Turn to page 89."

Have your student read the story "The Gum."

Read "The Sad Hog"

"In this next story, one of the characters goes to a bog. He sits right down on the muddy ground."

"A *bog* is an area that is wet and swampy."

"Say the word with me: *bog*."

_____

"If your best friend were sad, what would you do to cheer him or her up?" Discuss ways to cheer up a friend.

"In this story, a little girl tries to cheer up her sad pet. Turn to page 99."

Have your student read the story "The Sad Hog."

Read-Aloud Time

Read a Story or Poem

Read aloud to your student for twenty minutes.

Track Your Progress

Mark the Progress Chart

Have your student mark Lesson 13 on the Progress Chart.

Lesson 14 - Letters <u>qu</u> and <u>x</u>

This lesson will teach words containing the letters <u>qu</u> and <u>x</u>.

You will need: ☐ Phonogram Cards 25-26 ☐ Word Cards 73-78

☐ *Blast Off to Reading!* pages 51-55

Before You Begin

Preview the Sounds of the Letters

Listen to the *Phonogram Sounds* app for a demonstration of the phonogram sounds in today's lesson.

qu The letters <u>q</u> and <u>u</u> work together to make the /kw/ sound as in *queen*. In this phonogram, the <u>u</u> doesn't act like a vowel.

x The letter <u>x</u> says /ks/ as in *ax*.

Review

Review the Phonogram Cards that are behind the Review divider in your student's Reading Review Box. Show the card to your student and have him say the sound. If necessary, remind your student of the sound.

Review the Word Cards that are behind the Review divider in your student's Reading Review Box. If your student has difficulty reading the word, build the word with letter tiles and have your student sound it out using the procedure shown in Appendix C: Full Blending Procedure.

New Teaching

Teach New Letter Sounds

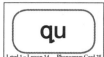

Hold up the Phonogram Card for the letters <u>qu</u>.

"See how there are two letters on one card? In English words, the letter <u>q</u> is always followed by the letter <u>u</u>. Together, these letters say /kw/. Repeat after me: /kw/." *Student repeats.*

Tip! Some students are helped by knowing that the sound of <u>x</u> is made by two sounds spoken in rapid succession: /k/ and /s/.

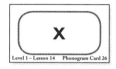

Hold up the Phonogram Card for the letter <u>x</u>.

"The letter <u>x</u> says /ks/. Repeat after me: /ks/." *Student repeats.*

File the Phonogram Cards behind the Review divider of the Reading Review Box.

Now practice the same sounds using the letter tiles. Pull these two letter tiles down into your work space. Point to each one in random order, and ask your student to tell you the sound that each tile makes.

qu x

Practice until your student can say the sound of each letter accurately.

Blend Sounds with Letter Tiles

Build the word *fix* with letter tiles. f i x

"I'll sound out this first word, and then you'll sound out the next word."

Touch the <u>f</u> and say /f/.

Touch the <u>i</u> and say /ĭ/.

Touch the <u>x</u> and say /ks/.

Now go back to the beginning of the word. Slide your finger under the letters <u>f</u>-<u>i</u>-<u>x</u> and say *fix* slowly.

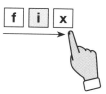

Finally, read the word *fix* at a normal pace, as we do when we speak.

Using the same procedure for blending, have your student sound out the word *quit*.

Play "Change the Word"

Keep the word *quit* on the board. | qu | i | t |

"I'm going to change the first letter of this word."

"What does this new word say?" Encourage your student to sound out the new word. *Fit.*

Continue to change one letter at a time to form the following words. Each time, have your student sound out the new word.

fit → it → is → as → has

ax → tax → wax

Return the letter tiles to their place in the alphabet.

Note that this is the first time you will be changing the vowel during this activity: *is – as*. You may wish to point this out to your student.

Also, your student has already learned that the letter <u>s</u> says two sounds. In the words *as* and *has*, <u>s</u> says its second sound.

New Teaching
(continued)

Complete Activity Sheet

What's in the Box?

Remove pages 51-52 from the *Blast Off* activity book.

Cut out each of the gift boxes, mix them up, and place them word-side down on a table.

To play, your student selects a gift box and turns it over to read the two-word phrase. If your student reads the phrase correctly, he can keep the gift box. If the phrase is read incorrectly, then the box is returned to the pile for another try.

Practice Reading Words

Have your student practice reading the words on Word Cards 73-78.

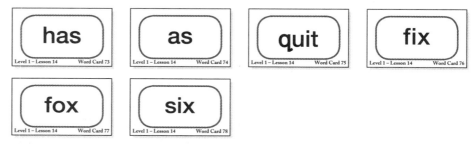

File the Word Cards behind the Review divider of the Reading Review Box.

New Teaching
(continued)

Practice Fluency

Remove pages 53-55 from the *Blast Off* activity book.

Have your student read from the Fluency Practice sheets.

Choppy Reading   Tip!

It is normal for beginning students to read choppily, one word at a time. They are working very hard at decoding each individual word, so don't expect smooth reading at this stage.

However, you can help your student advance to the next level of fluency in these two ways:

1. Have your student do a "cold reading" and then a "hot reading" of the sentences on the Fluency Practice sheet. The first time he reads through the sentences, it is a cold reading. Have him read the same sentences several more times to warm up and improve his fluency. When he thinks he is able to read the sentences smoothly, he can announce that he is ready to do a final "hot reading." Celebrate the difference between the cold reading and the hot reading.

2. Model fluency for your student. Read a sentence aloud with expression, and then have your student read the same sentence after you. This exercise accustoms the student to the feeling of reading at a faster, smoother pace.

At this beginning level, don't make a big deal about choppy reading. Just work toward the goal of fluency little by little, and recognize the hard work that your student is accomplishing.

Read-Aloud Time   Read a Story or Poem

Read aloud to your student for twenty minutes.

Track Your Progress

Mark the Progress Chart

Have your student mark Lesson 14 on the Progress Chart.

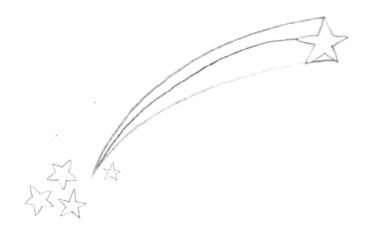

Lesson 15 - Read "Fox in a Box"

In this lesson, your student will apply what he has learned by reading a story.

You will need: ☐ *Run, Bug, Run!* book

Review

Review the Phonogram Cards that are behind the Review divider in your student's Reading Review Box. Show the card to your student and have him say the sound. If necessary, remind your student of the sound.

Review the Word Cards that are behind the Review divider in your student's Reading Review Box. If your student has difficulty reading the word, build the word with letter tiles and have your student sound it out using the procedure shown in Appendix C: Full Blending Procedure.

New Teaching

Read "Fox in a Box"

"Have you ever played with an empty box? What kinds of things can you do with a big box?" Discuss creative ways to play with a box.

"In the story you are about to read, a fox has lots of fun with a box. Turn to page 109."

Have your student read the story "Fox in a Box."

Read-Aloud Time

Read a Story or Poem

Read aloud to your student for twenty minutes.

Track Your Progress

Mark the Progress Chart

Have your student mark Lesson 15 on the Progress Chart.

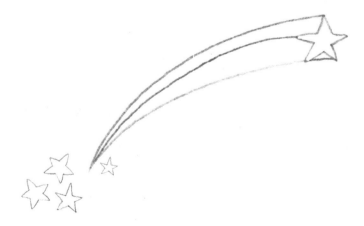

Lesson 16 - Consonant Team <u>th</u>

This lesson will teach words containing both sounds of consonant team <u>th</u>.

You will need:
- ☐ Phonogram Card 27
- ☐ Letter tile <u>th</u>
- ☐ Consonant Teams label
- ☐ *Blast Off to Reading!* pages 57-62
- ☐ Word Cards 79-85
- ☐ spatula

Before You Begin

Preview the Sounds of the Letters

Listen to the *Phonogram Sounds* app for a demonstration of the phonogram sounds in today's lesson.

th   Today you will be teaching the consonant team <u>th</u>. A consonant team is two letters that work together to make one sound. Other consonant teams include <u>sh</u>, <u>ch</u>, <u>ng</u>, and <u>ck</u>.

Depending on the word, <u>th</u> says /th/ as in *three* or /~~th~~/ as in *then*. You will notice that there is a strikethrough on the <u>th</u> in the second sound: /~~th~~/. The strikethrough is used to differentiate between the two sounds of <u>th</u>. The /~~th~~/ is considered a *voiced* sound because we use our vocal cords to say it, while the /th/ is considered an *unvoiced* sound.

Your student will learn both sounds for <u>th</u> in this lesson.

Place the Consonant Teams Label on the Board

We will use the Consonant Teams label to organize consonant teams like <u>th</u>. Place the label under the alphabet row, and the letter tile under the label.

| a | b | c | d | e | f | g | h | i | j | k | l | m | ... |

Consonant Teams

th

Review

Review the Phonogram Cards that are behind the Review divider in your student's Reading Review Box. Show the card to your student and have him say the sound. If necessary, remind your student of the sound.

Review the Word Cards that are behind the Review divider in your student's Reading Review Box. If your student has difficulty reading the word, build the word with letter tiles and have your student sound it out using the procedure shown in Appendix C: Full Blending Procedure.

New Teaching

Teach New Letter Sounds

Teach the Phonogram Card for the consonant team th.

"See how there are two letters on one card? The two letters work together to make one sound."

"These letters can say /th/, or they can say /t̶h̶/."

"Now it's your turn. What do these letters say?" *Student says /th/–/t̶h̶/.*

File the Phonogram Card behind the Review divider of the Reading Review Box.

Set out the new letter tile. | th |

"The letter tile for /th/–/t̶h̶/ also has both letters on it."

Practice with the letter tile until your student can say the sounds of th accurately.

Blend Sounds with Letter Tiles

"When we read words with th, we try the first sound first. If that doesn't make a word you recognize, then try the second sound of th."

Build the word *them* with letter tiles. | th | e | m |

"I'll sound out this first word, and then you'll sound out the next word."

New Teaching
(continued)

"First I try the first sound of <u>th</u>." Touch the <u>th</u> and say /th/.

"Then I sound out the rest of the word."

Touch the <u>e</u> and say /ĕ/, then touch the <u>m</u> and say /m/.

Now go back to the beginning of the word and blend the sounds together, using the first sound of <u>th</u>. Slide your finger under the letters <u>th</u>-<u>e</u>-<u>m</u> and say /thĕm/.

"With the first sound of <u>th</u>, this word doesn't sound like a word I recognize. So now I try the second sound of <u>th</u>, /t̶h̶/."

Repeat the steps above, using the second sound of <u>th</u>. Then go back and blend the sounds together. Slide your finger under the letters <u>th</u>-<u>e</u>-<u>m</u> and say *them*.

"So this word says *them*. It uses /t̶h̶/, the second sound of <u>th</u>."

"Now it's your turn. Remember to always try the first sound of <u>th</u> first."

Using the same procedure for blending, have your student sound out the words *this* and *bath*. Be sure the student tries the first sound of <u>th</u> first, then the second sound.

Play "Change the Word"

Keep the word *bath* on the board.

"I'm going to change the first letter of this word."

New Teaching
(continued)

"What does this new word say?" Encourage your student to sound out the new word. *Math.*

Continue to change one letter at a time to form the following words. Each time, have your student sound out the new word.

math → path → pat → pan → than → an → in → thin

Return the letter tiles to their place in the alphabet.

ended here 1/16/17 -Lucie

Complete Activity Sheet

Over Easy
Remove pages 57-60 from the *Blast Off* activity book.

Cut out the eggs. Color the yolks yellow, if desired.

Place several eggs sunny side up in a pan.

Have your student use a spatula to flip over the eggs, one at a time, and read the word.

If your student reads the word correctly, he can keep the fried egg. If he reads the word incorrectly, put the egg back in the pan and retry.

Practice Reading Words

Have your student practice reading the words on Word Cards 79-85.

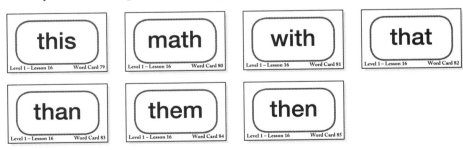

File the Word Cards behind the Review divider of the Reading Review Box.

Lesson 16: Consonant Team <u>th</u>

New Teaching
(continued)

Practice Fluency

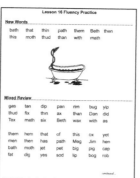

Remove pages 61-62 from the *Blast Off* activity book.

Have your student read from the Fluency Practice sheets.

Avoid Making Corrections Too Soon

Tip!

Find a balance between correcting reading mistakes promptly and correcting mistakes too quickly.

When your student misreads a word in a sentence, resist the temptation to correct the misread word immediately. Let him reach the end of the sentence before interrupting, giving him the chance to realize on his own that he made a mistake.

For example, if the student reads *The hot sat with a thud*, he will probably self-correct because the sentence obviously doesn't make sense. He will look back to see where his error is, and reread the sentence as *The hog sat with a thud*. If he does continue reading without correcting himself, ask him if the sentence he just read makes sense.

Interrupting a student immediately after he makes an error deprives him of the opportunity to monitor what he is reading for meaning. The phrase *The hot...* does make sense in itself, as it could be *The hot day* or *The hot lunch*. If you give your student time to reach the end of the sentence, though, it will most likely be clear to him that he has misread a word.

Read-Aloud Time   Read a Story or Poem

Read aloud to your student for twenty minutes.

Track Your Progress   Mark the Progress Chart

Have your student mark Lesson 16 on the Progress Chart.

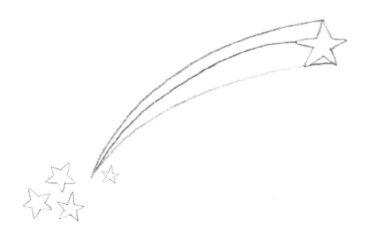

Lesson 16: Consonant Team <u>th</u>

Lesson 17 - Read "The Red Pen"

In this lesson, your student will apply what he has learned by reading a story.

You will need: ☐ *Run, Bug, Run!* book

Review

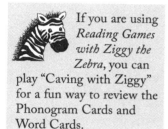 If you are using *Reading Games with Ziggy the Zebra,* you can play "Caving with Ziggy" for a fun way to review the Phonogram Cards and Word Cards.

 Review the Phonogram Cards that are behind the Review divider in your student's Reading Review Box. Show the card to your student and have him say the sound. If necessary, remind your student of the sound.

 Review the Word Cards that are behind the Review divider in your student's Reading Review Box. If your student has difficulty reading the word, build the word with letter tiles and have your student sound it out using the procedure shown in Appendix C: Full Blending Procedure.

New Teaching

Read "The Red Pen"

"If you could be anything for a day, like a bird or a tree or a cloud, what would you be?" Discuss what your student would do during his day as his chosen object.

"The boy in the story you are about to read has a big imagination. Let's see what he would like to be. Turn to page 121."

Have your student read the story "The Red Pen."

Read-Aloud Time

Read a Story or Poem

Read aloud to your student for twenty minutes.

Track Your Progress

Mark the Progress Chart

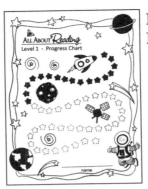

Have your student mark Lesson 17 on the Progress Chart.

Lesson 17: Read "The Red Pen"

Lesson 18 - Consonant Team sh

This lesson will teach words containing the consonant team sh.

You will need: ☐ Phonogram Card 28   ☐ *Blast Off to Reading!* pages 63-71

☐ Letter tile sh   ☐ Word Cards 86-90

Before You Begin

Preview the Sounds of the Letters

Listen to the *Phonogram Sounds* app for a demonstration of the phonogram sound in today's lesson.

sh   The consonant team sh says /sh/ as in *ship*.

Place the sh tile under the Consonant Teams label.

Review

Review the Phonogram Cards that are behind the Review divider in your student's Reading Review Box. Show the card to your student and have him say the sound. If necessary, remind your student of the sound.

Review the Word Cards that are behind the Review divider in your student's Reading Review Box. If your student has difficulty reading the word, build the word with letter tiles and have your student sound it out using the procedure shown in Appendix C: Full Blending Procedure.

New Teaching

Teach New Letter Sounds

Teach the Phonogram Card for the consonant team <u>sh</u>.

Level 1 – Lesson 18   Phonogram Card 28

1. Hold up the Phonogram Card and say the sound.
2. Have your student repeat the sound.

File the Phonogram Card behind the Review divider of the Reading Review Box.

Set out the new letter tile. Practice with the tile until your student can say the sound accurately. sh

Blend Sounds with Letter Tiles

Build the word *shut* with letter tiles. sh u t

"I'll sound out this first word, and then you'll sound out the next word."

Touch the <u>sh</u> and say */sh/*.

Touch the <u>u</u> and say */ŭ/*.

Touch the <u>t</u> and say */t/*.

Lesson 18: Consonant Team <u>sh</u>

Now go back to the beginning of the word. Slide your finger under the letters <u>sh</u>-<u>u</u>-<u>t</u> and say *shut* slowly.

Finally, read the word *shut* at a normal pace, as we do when we speak.

Using the same procedure for blending, have your student sound out the word *cash*.

| c | a | sh |

Play "Change the Word"

Build the word *wish*. | w | i | sh |

"What is this word?" *Wish*.

"I'm going to change the first letter of this word."

"What does this new word say?" Encourage your student to sound out the new word. *Fish*.

Continue to change one letter at a time to form the following words. Each time, have your student sound out the new word.

fish → dish → dip → ship → shop

Return the letter tiles to their place in the alphabet.

New Teaching
(continued)

Complete Activity Sheet

Word Flipper

Remove pages 63-68 from the *Blast Off* activity book.

Follow the assembly instructions on page 59 of Lesson 6.

Have your student flip through the book randomly, reading both the real and the nonsense words that are formed.

Practice Reading Words

Have your student practice reading the words on Word Cards 86-90.

File the Word Cards behind the Review divider of the Reading Review Box.

Lesson 18: Consonant Team <u>sh</u>

New Teaching
(continued)

Practice Fluency

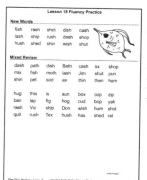

Remove pages 69-71 from the *Blast Off* activity book.

Have your student read from the Fluency Practice sheets.

Avoid Excessive Feedback

Tip!

In the Fluency Practice tip in Lesson 16, we talked about why it is important to let your student finish the sentence even after he has misread a word. This practice encourages the student to monitor for meaning, asking himself "Does this sentence make sense?"

On the flip side of the coin is the teacher who offers immediate feedback, constantly interrupting the student for every misread word. Too often, such a stream of feedback causes the student to become dependent on the teacher to confirm that the word or phrase he just read is correct. The reader waits for the teacher to nod or say "good" or "uh-huh," which then becomes a cycle: the student reads a word or two, waits for affirmation, then reads a few more words. This stop-and-go cycle works against the development of fluency.

If you feel yourself falling into this negative routine with your student, let him know that from now on, you will give feedback after the sentence has been completed, instead of during his reading.

Lesson 18: Consonant Team <u>sh</u>

Read-Aloud Time   Read a Story or Poem

Read aloud to your student for twenty minutes.

Track Your Progress

Mark the Progress Chart

Have your student mark Lesson 18 on the Progress Chart.

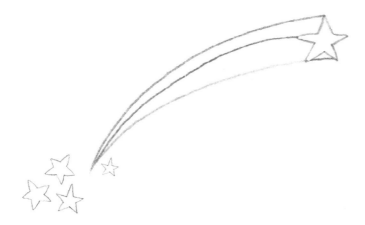

Lesson 19 - Read "Six Fish"

In this lesson, your student will apply what he has learned by reading a story.

You will need: ☐ *Run, Bug, Run!* book

Review

Review the Phonogram Cards that are behind the Review divider in your student's Reading Review Box. Show the card to your student and have him say the sound. If necessary, remind your student of the sound.

Review the Word Cards that are behind the Review divider in your student's Reading Review Box. If your student has difficulty reading the word, build the word with letter tiles and have your student sound it out using the procedure shown in Appendix C: Full Blending Procedure.

New Teaching

Read "Six Fish"

"What kind of animal do you think makes the best pet?" Discuss your student's chosen animal and why it makes a good pet.

"Let's see what kind of pet the girl in this story chooses. Turn to page 135."

Have your student read the story "Six Fish."

Read-Aloud Time

Read a Story or Poem

Read aloud to your student for twenty minutes.

Track Your Progress

Mark the Progress Chart

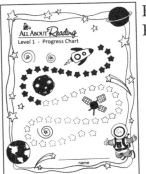

Have your student mark Lesson 19 on the Progress Chart.

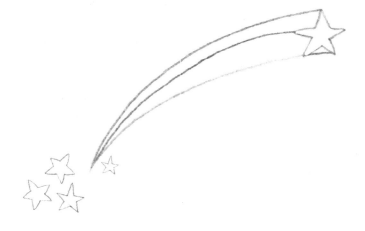

Lesson 19: Read "Six Fish"

Lesson 20 - Consonant Team <u>ch</u>

This lesson will teach words containing the consonant team <u>ch</u>.

You will need: ☐ Phonogram Card 29   ☐ *Blast Off to Reading!* pages 73-79
☐ Letter tile <u>ch</u>   ☐ Word Cards 91-94

Before You Begin

Preview the Sounds of the Letters

Listen to the *Phonogram Sounds* app for a demonstration of the phonogram sounds in today's lesson.

<u>ch</u> The consonant team <u>ch</u> has three different sounds: /ch/–/k/–/sh/. In this lesson, your student will learn the first and most common sound, /ch/ as in *child*. The other two sounds will be taught in Lesson 46.

Place the <u>ch</u> tile under the Consonant Teams label.

Review

Review the Phonogram Cards that are behind the Review divider in your student's Reading Review Box. Show the card to your student and have him say the sound. If necessary, remind your student of the sound.

Review the Word Cards that are behind the Review divider in your student's Reading Review Box. If your student has difficulty reading the word, build the word with letter tiles and have your student sound it out using the procedure shown in Appendix C: Full Blending Procedure.

New Teaching

Teach New Letter Sounds

Teach the Phonogram Card for the consonant team <u>ch</u>.

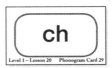

1. Hold up the Phonogram Card and say the sound.
2. Have your student repeat the sound.

File the Phonogram Card behind the Review divider of the Reading Review Box.

Set out the new letter tile. Practice with the tile until your student can say the sound accurately. ch

Blend Sounds with Letter Tiles

Build the word *chop* with letter tiles. ch o p

"I'll sound out this first word, and then you'll sound out the next word."

Touch the <u>ch</u> and say /*ch*/. ch o p

Touch the <u>o</u> and say /ŏ/. ch o p

Touch the <u>p</u> and say /*p*/. ch o p

New Teaching
(continued)

Now go back to the beginning of the word. Slide your finger under the letters ch-o-p and say *chop* slowly.

Finally, read the word *chop* at a normal pace, as we do when we speak.

Using the same procedure for blending, have your student sound out the word *rich*.

| r | i | ch |

Play "Change the Word"

Build the word *chin*. | ch | i | n |

"What is this word?" *Chin*.

"I'm going to change the last letter of this word."

"What does this new word say?" Encourage your student to sound out the new word. *Chip*.

Continue to change one letter at a time to form the following words. Each time, have your student sound out the new word.

chip → chop

Return the letter tiles to their place in the alphabet.

Complete Activity Sheet

<u>Little Mouse</u>
Remove pages 73-76 from the *Blast Off* activity book.

Color the cheese and mouse, if desired. Cut out the mouse, and cut the cheese into twelve pieces, as indicated.

Set out the twelve pieces of cheese with the words facing down.

You and your student take turns being the mouse. The mouse sneaks up to the pile of cheese and takes one piece.

The mouse reads the word on the piece of cheese that was selected. If the word is read correctly, the mouse keeps the cheese. If the word is read incorrectly, it goes back into the cheese pile.

Practice Reading Words

Have your student practice reading the words on Word Cards 91-94.

File the Word Cards behind the Review divider of the Reading Review Box.

Lesson 20: Consonant Team <u>ch</u>

New Teaching
(continued)

Practice Fluency

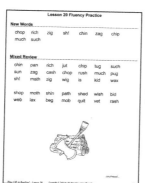

Remove pages 77-79 from the *Blast Off* activity book.

Have your student read from the Fluency Practice sheets.

Today's fluency practice includes a dash (—). Explain that a dash is a line that indicates a pause in speech or an unfinished sentence. Dashes can be used in the middle or at the end of a sentence.

Tip!

Read-Aloud Time

Read a Story or Poem

Read aloud to your student for twenty minutes.

Track Your Progress

Mark the Progress Chart

Have your student mark Lesson 20 on the Progress Chart.

Lesson 20: Consonant Team <u>ch</u>

Lesson 21 - Read "Get the Moth, Meg!"

In this lesson, your student will apply what he has learned by reading a story.

You will need: ☐ *Run, Bug, Run!* book

Review

Review the Phonogram Cards that are behind the Review divider in your student's Reading Review Box. Show the card to your student and have him say the sound. If necessary, remind your student of the sound.

Review the Word Cards that are behind the Review divider in your student's Reading Review Box. If your student has difficulty reading the word, build the word with letter tiles and have your student sound it out using the procedure shown in Appendix C: Full Blending Procedure.

Shuffle the cards behind the **Mastered** dividers and choose a selection for review.

New Teaching

Read "Get the Moth, Meg!"

"Did you ever have a mosquito or fly that just wouldn't leave you alone? Maybe it kept buzzing around your head! What could you do to try to catch it?" Discuss your student's experience and how he could catch the insect.

"Let's see what happens when the girl in this story tries to catch a moth. Turn to page 145."

Have your student read the story "Get the Moth, Meg!"

When you get to page 149, you may need to explain that *tap* is another word for faucet.

Read-Aloud Time Read a Story or Poem

Read aloud to your student for twenty minutes.

Track Your Progress

Mark the Progress Chart

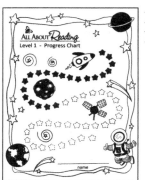

Have your student mark Lesson 21 on the Progress Chart.

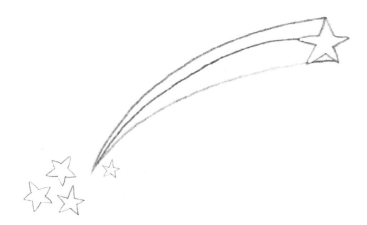

Lesson 21: Read "Get the Moth, Meg!"

Lesson 22 - Words with Final Blends

This lesson will teach words containing consonant blends at the end, as well as the sight word <u>was</u>.

You will need: ☐ *Blast Off to Reading!* pages 81-94

☐ Word Cards 95-104

Before You Begin

Understanding Consonant Blends

In this lesson, your student will learn to read words with consonant blends.

A consonant blend consists of two sounds that are said together quickly. For example, the word *lamp* has a consonant blend at the end. The /m/ and /p/ sounds are said in rapid succession, but each consonant keeps its own sound.

A blend at the end of a word is called a **final blend**. Final blends are easier to read than blends at the beginning of the word, so final blends are introduced first.

Words with consonant blends will be decoded using the same procedure that your student is already using. Touch each letter and say its sound, slowly at first, and then fast like a spoken word.

Review

Review the Phonogram Cards that are behind the Review divider in your student's Reading Review Box. Show the card to your student and have him say the sound. If necessary, remind your student of the sound.

Review the Word Cards that are behind the Review divider in your student's Reading Review Box. If your student has difficulty reading the word, build the word with letter tiles and have your student sound it out using the procedure shown in Appendix C: Full Blending Procedure.

New Teaching

Blend Sounds with Letter Tiles

Build the word *land* with letter tiles. | l | **a** | n | d |

"Sometimes there are two consonants at the end of a word, as in the word *land*. Listen and watch as I blend the letters in this word: l-a-n-d."

Touch the l and say /l/.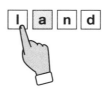

Touch the a and say /ă/.

Touch the n and say /n/.

Touch the d and say /d/.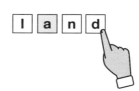

Now go back to the beginning of the word. Slide your finger under the letters l-a-n-d and say *land* slowly.

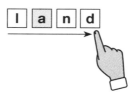

Finally, read the word *land* at a normal pace, as we do when we speak.

Using the same procedure for blending, have your student sound out the word *best*.

| b | e | s | t |

Give your student practice with blending these words that also contain two-letter phonograms:

| l | u | n | ch | | t | e | n | th |

New Teaching
(continued)

Complete Activity Sheets

Word Flipper

Remove pages 81-87 from the *Blast Off* activity book.

Each page will create one flipper. There are four Word Flippers in this lesson.

Cut apart the pages on the dotted lines.

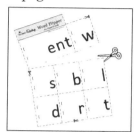

Put the larger pieces of paper on the bottom. Stack the smaller pieces on top, on the left side.

Staple the Word Flipper along the left side.

Have your student turn the pages and read the words that are formed.

Matching Socks

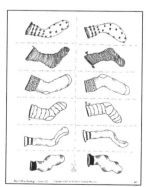

Remove pages 89-90 from the *Blast Off* activity book.

Cut out the individual socks and put them in random order on the table, with the words facing down.

Have your student find two socks that match, and then read the words on the back of the socks.

Practice Reading Words

Have your student practice reading the words on Word Cards 95-103.

File the Word Cards behind the Review divider of the Reading Review Box.

Teach a Sight Word: *was*

Show Word Card 104 to your student.

"Most words follow the rules and say the sounds that we expect them to say. But there are a few words that do not. Here is one of those words."

"This word is *was*, as in *She was a lion tamer.*"

Review this word several times today and then file it behind the Review divider.

New Teaching
(continued)

Practice Fluency

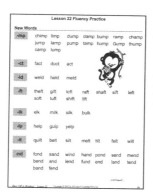

Remove pages 91-94 from the *Blast Off* activity book.

Have your student read from the Fluency Practice sheets.

Automatic Word Recognition

Tip!

Automatic word recognition means that words are recognized at a glance. If you have automatic word recognition, you don't have to decode the word; you just know what the word is with a single look. Another name for this skill is *automaticity*.

These fluency exercises give your student the practice he needs to develop automaticity. After encountering the same words multiple times, your student will move from sounding out the words to automatic word recognition.

Automaticity enables your student to read more fluently. When he doesn't have to laboriously decode each and every word, he can read smoothly and with more comprehension.

Read-Aloud Time

Read a Story or Poem

Read aloud to your student for twenty minutes.

Lesson 22: Words with Final Blends

Track Your Progress

Mark the Progress Chart

Have your student mark Lesson 22 on the Progress Chart.

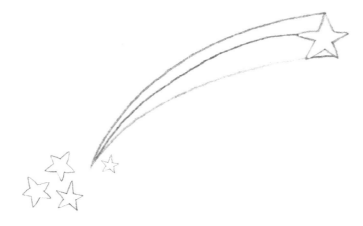

Lesson 23 - Read "Lost in the Bog"

In this lesson, your student will apply what he has learned by reading a story.

You will need: ☐ *The Runt Pig* book

Review

Review the Phonogram Cards that are behind the Review divider in your student's Reading Review Box. Show the card to your student and have him say the sound. If necessary, remind your student of the sound.

Review the Word Cards that are behind the Review divider in your student's Reading Review Box. If your student has difficulty reading the word, build the word with letter tiles and have your student sound it out using the procedure shown in Appendix C: Full Blending Procedure.

New Teaching

Read "Lost in the Bog"

"Have you ever seen a turtle? What do turtles do when they get scared? What do *you* do when you get scared?" Discuss how turtles hide in their shells, and what your student does when he is afraid of something.

"Let's see what happens when the turtle in this story gets scared. Turn to page 9."

Have your student read the story "Lost in the Bog."

Read-Aloud Time

Read a Story or Poem

Read aloud to your student for twenty minutes.

Track Your Progress

Mark the Progress Chart

Have your student mark Lesson 23 on the Progress Chart.

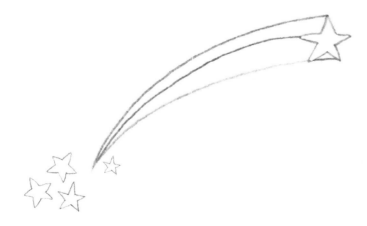

Lesson 24 - Words with Initial Blends

This lesson will teach words containing blends at the beginning, as well as the sight word _to_.

You will need: ☐ _Blast Off to Reading!_ pages 95-108

☐ Word Cards 105-114

Review

Review the Phonogram Cards that are behind the Review divider in your student's Reading Review Box. Show the card to your student and have him say the sound. If necessary, remind your student of the sound.

Review the Word Cards that are behind the Review divider in your student's Reading Review Box. If your student has difficulty reading the word, build the word with letter tiles and have your student sound it out using the procedure shown in Appendix C: Full Blending Procedure.

New Teaching

Blend Sounds with Letter Tiles

Build the word _spot_ with letter tiles. [s] [p] [o] [t]

"Sometimes there are two consonants at the beginning of a word, as in the word _spot_. Listen and watch as I blend the letters in this word: s-p-o-t."

Touch the s and say /s/.

Touch the p and say /p/.

Touch the <u>o</u> and say /ŏ/.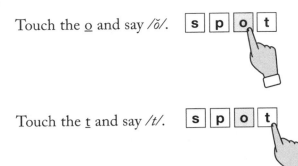

Touch the <u>t</u> and say /t/.

Now go back to the beginning of the word. Slide your finger under the letters <u>s</u>-<u>p</u>-<u>o</u>-<u>t</u> and say *spot* slowly.

Finally, read the word *spot* at a normal pace, as we do when we speak.

Using the same procedure for blending, have your student sound out the word *flag*.

| f | l | a | g |

Give your student practice with blending these words that also contain two-letter phonograms:

| th | r | o | b | | sh | r | e | d |

Complete Activity Sheets

Word Flipper

Remove pages 95-101 from the *Blast Off* activity book.

Each page will create one flipper. There are four Word Flippers in this lesson.

See the assembly instructions on page 125 of Lesson 22. For this lesson, however, the Word Flippers will be stapled on the right instead of on the left.

Have your student turn the pages and read the words that are formed.

How Animals Move

Remove page 103 from the *Blast Off* activity book.

Have your student match the picture of each animal with the movement it makes:

- *hop*   (frog, grasshopper)
- *trot*   (horse, zebra)
- *swim*   (fish)

New Teaching
(continued)

Practice Reading Words

Have your student practice reading the words on Word Cards 105-113.

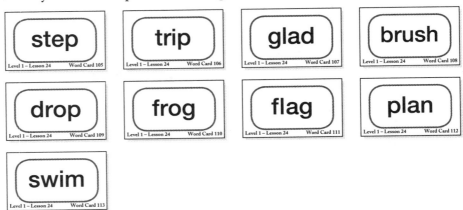

File the Word Cards behind the Review divider of the Reading Review Box.

Teach a Sight Word: *to*

We are treating the word *to* as a sight word because it contains the third sound of <u>o</u>, which has not been taught yet.

"Today we have one word that doesn't say what we expect it to say."

Show Word Card 114 to your student.

"This word is *to*, as in *Did you go to the lake?*"

Review this word several times today and then file it behind the Review divider.

Lesson 24: Words with Initial Blends

New Teaching
(continued)

Practice Fluency

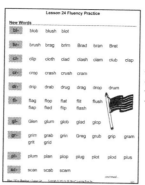

Remove pages 105-108 from the *Blast Off* activity book.

Have your student read from the Fluency Practice sheets.

Read-Aloud Time

Read a Story or Poem

Read aloud to your student for twenty minutes.

Track Your Progress

Mark the Progress Chart

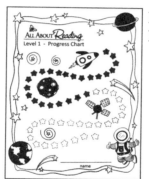

Have your student mark Lesson 24 on the Progress Chart.

Lesson 24: Words with Initial Blends

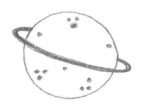

Lesson 25 - Read "The Big Top"

In this lesson, your student will apply what he has learned by reading a story.

You will need: ☐ *The Runt Pig* book

Review

Review the Phonogram Cards that are behind the Review divider in your student's Reading Review Box. Show the card to your student and have him say the sound. If necessary, remind your student of the sound.

Review the Word Cards that are behind the Review divider in your student's Reading Review Box. If your student has difficulty reading the word, build the word with letter tiles and have your student sound it out using the procedure shown in Appendix C: Full Blending Procedure.

New Teaching

Read "The Big Top"

"Have you ever seen a circus? Sometimes a circus is held in a great big tent that is called 'the big top.' What kinds of things can you see at a circus?" Discuss the different people and animals at a circus, such as clowns, horses, elephants, and trapeze artists.

"The story you are going to read is about all the things you can see at a circus. Turn to page 23."

Have your student read the story "The Big Top."

Read-Aloud Time

Read a Story or Poem

Read aloud to your student for twenty minutes.

Track Your Progress

Mark the Progress Chart

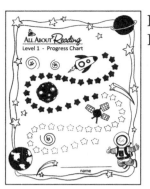

Have your student mark Lesson 25 on the Progress Chart.

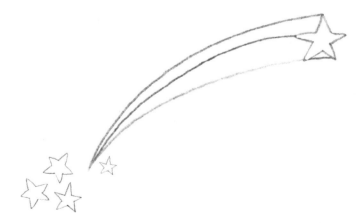

Lesson 25: Read "The Big Top"

Lesson 26 - FF, LL, and SS

This lesson will teach words ending in <u>ff</u>, <u>ll</u>, and <u>ss</u>, as well as the sight words <u>said</u> and <u>I</u>.

You will need: ☐ *Blast Off to Reading!* pages 109-120

☐ Extra <u>f</u>, <u>l</u>, and <u>s</u> letter tiles

☐ Word Cards 115-124

Before You Begin

Organize the Extra Letter Tiles

Take out the extra <u>f</u>, <u>l</u>, and <u>s</u> tiles. Place them on the board as follows:

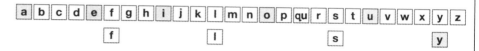

The letters <u>f</u>, <u>l</u>, and <u>s</u> are often doubled after a single vowel at the end of a one-syllable word.

Review

Review the Phonogram Cards that are behind the Review divider in your student's Reading Review Box. Show the card to your student and have him say the sound. If necessary, remind your student of the sound.

Review the Word Cards that are behind the Review divider in your student's Reading Review Box. If your student has difficulty reading the word, build the word with letter tiles and have your student sound it out using the procedure shown in Appendix C: Full Blending Procedure.

New Teaching

Blend Sounds with Letter Tiles

Build the word *stiff* with letter tiles. | s | t | i | f | f |

"Sometimes there are two of the same letter at the end of a word, like in the word *stiff*. Listen and watch as I blend the letters in this word: s-t-i-f."

Touch the s and say */s/*.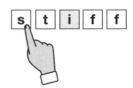

Touch the t and say */t/*.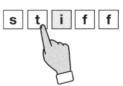

Touch the i and say */ĭ/*.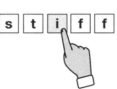

Touch the two f's and say */f/*.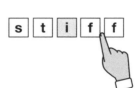

Now go back to the beginning of the word. Slide your finger under the letters s-t-i-f-f and say *stiff* slowly.

Finally, read the word *stiff* at a normal pace, as we do when we speak.

"When we see two of the same letters at the end of a word like this, we only have to pronounce it once. We wouldn't say *stiff-ff* because that would sound funny."

Using the same procedure for blending, have your student sound out the words *glass* and *bill*.

| g | l | a | s | s | | b | i | l | l |

New Teaching
(continued)

Complete Activity Sheets

Word Flipper

Remove pages 109-113 from the *Blast Off* activity book.

Each page will create one flipper. There are three Word Flippers in this lesson.

See the assembly instructions on page 125 of Lesson 22.

Have your student turn the pages and read the words that are formed.

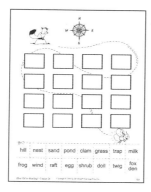

Compass Points

Remove page 115 from the *Blast Off* activity book.

Cut out the sixteen game cards from the bottom of the sheet and place one on each square of the game board, face down.

Give your student a marker, such as an M&M, small wad of paper, or coin.

To begin the game, place the marker on the first square just below Frisky Fox.

"Frisky Fox is chasing a dragonfly. Follow Frisky to see what she sees."

"Go east one square." *Student moves the marker east one square, turns over the game card, and reads the word.*

If the student reads the word correctly, he keeps the card. Otherwise, the card is returned to the board.

"Go south two squares." *Student moves the marker south two squares, turns over both game cards, and reads the word.*

Continue giving directions until every game card has been read.

 Tip!

Explain the compass on the activity sheet to your student. Have him point to North, South, East, and West on the compass.

You may wish to teach a mnemonic to help your student remember the order of the compass points. Here are common sayings to help remember the clockwise position of North, East, South, and West.

<u>N</u>ever <u>E</u>at <u>S</u>hredded <u>W</u>heat
<u>N</u>ever <u>E</u>at <u>S</u>oggy <u>W</u>affles
<u>N</u>aughty <u>E</u>lephants <u>S</u>quirt <u>W</u>ater
<u>N</u>ever <u>E</u>at <u>S</u>limy <u>W</u>orms

Lesson 26: FF, LL, and SS

141

New Teaching
(continued)

Practice Reading Words

Have your student practice reading the words on Word Cards 115-122.

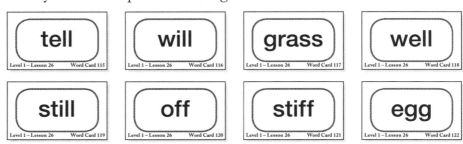

File the Word Cards behind the Review divider of the Reading Review Box.

Teach Two Sight Words: *said* and *I*

Show Word Card 123 to your student.

"Most words follow the rules and say the sounds that we expect them to say. But there are a few words that do not. Here is one of those words."

"This word is *said*, as in *She said hello*."

Show Word Card 124 to your student.

"This word is *I*, as in *I am a student*. The word *I* is always spelled with a capital i."

Review these words several times today and then file them behind the Review divider.

We are treating the word *I* as a sight word because it contains the long sound of i, which has not been taught yet.

New Teaching
(continued)

Practice Fluency

Remove pages 117-120 from the *Blast Off* activity book.

Have your student read the New Words section of the Fluency Practice sheets.

Point to the words under the More New Words section. "Today you learned that the letters <u>f</u>, <u>l</u>, and <u>s</u> are often doubled at the end of a word. Sometimes other letters are doubled at the end of a word, too, as in the words *fizz* and *egg*."

Have your student read the words in the More New Words section, and then continue with the remaining sections.

Direct Quotations

The word *said* is used quite often in books where there is a lot of dialogue. Consider these examples:
- My brother said, "The turtle bit me!"
- "I told you to keep your fingers out of his cage!" said Mom.

When we talk, we normally use the noun-verb pattern, as in *Frank said, "Let's eat."* But in books, authors usually use the verb-noun pattern, as in *"Let's eat," said Frank.*

Because you have been reading aloud to your student every day, he should be used to hearing this verb-noun pattern. Today's Fluency Practice sheet will give your student practice with reading direct quotations.

Lesson 26: FF, LL, and SS

Read-Aloud Time   Read a Story or Poem

Read aloud to your student for twenty minutes.

Track Your Progress

Mark the Progress Chart

Have your student mark Lesson 26 on the Progress Chart.

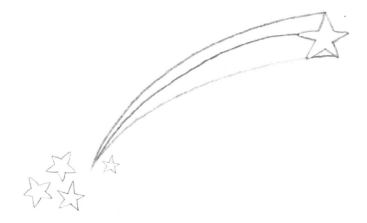

Lesson 27 - Read "Slim Went West" and "Mud Milk"

In this lesson, your student will apply what he has learned by reading two stories.

You will need: ☐ *The Runt Pig* book

Review

Review the Phonogram Cards that are behind the Review divider in your student's Reading Review Box. Show the card to your student and have him say the sound. If necessary, remind your student of the sound.

Review the Word Cards that are behind the Review divider in your student's Reading Review Box. If your student has difficulty reading the word, build the word with letter tiles and have your student sound it out using the procedure shown in Appendix C: Full Blending Procedure.

New Teaching

Read "Slim Went West"

"In this next story, Slim decides to go out West to a *vast* land. He takes out his map and sees a big area that has not yet been settled."

"If something is *vast*, it is *very big*."

"Say the word with me: *vast*."

"The *ocean* is vast. If you are in the middle of an ocean, it feels like it will go on and on forever. You can look in all directions, and all you can see is water."

"The *desert* is another vast place. You can look in all directions, and all you can see is sand."

"What is the opposite of *vast*?" Possible answers: *small, tiny, not large.*

New Teaching
(continued)

"If you could go on a trip, where would you go?" Discuss where your student would go, and mention whether the destination is east, west, north, or south.

"The man in this story has a big adventure in the West. Turn to page 37."

Have your student read the story "Slim Went West."

Read "Mud Milk"

"When you are thirsty, what tastes really good to you?"

"Sometimes when people like the taste of something, they say it really hits the spot. Let's see what hits the spot for the girl in this story. Turn to page 53."

Have your student read the poem "Mud Milk."

Read-Aloud Time

Read a Story or Poem

Read aloud to your student for twenty minutes.

Track Your Progress

Mark the Progress Chart

Have your student mark Lesson 27 on the Progress Chart.

Lesson 28 - Read "The Wind on the Hill" and "The Ant Hill"

In this lesson, your student will apply what he has learned by reading two stories.

You will need: ☐ *The Runt Pig* book

Review

Review the Phonogram Cards that are behind the Review divider in your student's Reading Review Box. Show the card to your student and have him say the sound. If necessary, remind your student of the sound.

Review the Word Cards that are behind the Review divider in your student's Reading Review Box. If your student has difficulty reading the word, build the word with letter tiles and have your student sound it out using the procedure shown in Appendix C: Full Blending Procedure.

Shuffle the cards behind the **Mastered** dividers and choose a selection for review.

If your student has any difficulties in reading the next two stories, review the fluency sections of the previous lessons.

New Teaching

Read "The Wind on the Hill"

"Sometimes clouds make funny shapes in the sky. What do fluffy white clouds look like to you? What about dark clouds?" Discuss your student's ideas about clouds.

"In this next story, a boy and a girl see lots of things in the clouds. Turn to page 61."

Have your student read the story "The Wind on the Hill."

Read "The Ant Hill"

"Have you ever observed ants working on an ant hill? They are very busy, aren't they? What do you see ants do as they work?" Discuss how ants climb and carry bits of dirt and grass.

"The ants in the next story work very hard. Let's see what they are building. Turn to page 75."

Have your student read the story "The Ant Hill."

Read-Aloud Time

Read a Story or Poem

Read aloud to your student for twenty minutes.

Track Your Progress

Mark the Progress Chart

Have your student mark Lesson 28 on the Progress Chart.

Lesson 29 - Two Sight Words

This lesson will teach the sight words <u>for</u> and <u>no</u>.

You will need: ☐ *Blast Off to Reading!* pages 121-122

☐ *Word Cards 125-126*

Review

Review the Phonogram Cards that are behind the Review divider in your student's Reading Review Box. Show the card to your student and have him say the sound. If necessary, remind your student of the sound.

Review the Word Cards that are behind the Review divider in your student's Reading Review Box. If your student has difficulty reading the word, build the word with letter tiles and have your student sound it out using the procedure shown in Appendix C: Full Blending Procedure.

New Teaching

Teach Two Sight Words: *for* and *no*

"Today we have two words that don't say what we expect them to say."

Show Word Card 125 to your student.

"This word is *for*, as in *I have a surprise for you.*"

Show Word Card 126 to your student.

"This word is *no*, as in *There are no more cookies.*"

Review these words several times today and then file them behind the Review divider.

We are treating *for* as a sight word because it contains the phonogram <u>or</u>, which has not been taught yet.

The word *no* is also treated as a sight word at this stage because long vowels have not been taught yet.

Practice Fluency

Remove pages 121-122 from the *Blast Off* activity book.

Have your student read from the Fluency Practice sheets.

Vocabulary Affects Fluency

Tip!

If you've ever picked up a book outside of your expertise (such as a medical book if you are an architect, or an engineering book if you are a horticulturist), then you've encountered unfamiliar vocabulary words that you don't understand. It would be difficult for you to read these books fluently because you wouldn't know what many of the words mean or how to pronounce them.

In the same way, it is difficult for your student to read fluently if he doesn't understand what the words mean. You can help your student develop a large listening vocabulary by reading aloud from a wide selection of books and discussing unfamiliar words.

Read-Aloud Time   Read a Story or Poem

Read aloud to your student for twenty minutes.

Track Your Progress   Mark the Progress Chart

Have your student mark Lesson 29 on the Progress Chart.

Lesson 30 - Read "The Hit" and "Fish Class"

In this lesson, your student will apply what he has learned by reading two stories.

You will need: ☐ *The Runt Pig* book

Review

Review the Phonogram Cards that are behind the Review divider in your student's Reading Review Box. Show the card to your student and have him say the sound. If necessary, remind your student of the sound.

Review the Word Cards that are behind the Review divider in your student's Reading Review Box. If your student has difficulty reading the word, build the word with letter tiles and have your student sound it out using the procedure shown in Appendix C: Full Blending Procedure.

If your student has any difficulties in reading the next two stories, review the fluency sections of the previous lessons.

New Teaching

Read "The Hit"

In the next three lessons, your student will be reading a selection of stories that contain blends.

"Have you ever lost something you really liked? Where did you look for it? Did you ever find it?" Discuss your student's lost item and if and how he found it.

"Let's see what happens when the boys in this story lose their baseball. Turn to page 87."

Have your student read the story "The Hit."

New Teaching (continued)	## Read "Fish Class"

"Pretend you are a fish in the lake and you go to school. What kinds of lessons do you think little fish have to learn? What would be your favorite lesson as a fish?" Discuss your student's ideas.

"Let's see what kinds of things the fish in this story learn. Turn to page 101."

Have your student read the story "Fish Class."

Read-Aloud Time	## Read a Story or Poem

Read aloud to your student for twenty minutes.

Track Your Progress	## Mark the Progress Chart

 Have your student mark Lesson 30 on the Progress Chart.

Lesson 31 - Read "The Big Mess" and "The Plan"

In this lesson, your student will apply what he has learned by reading two stories.

You will need: ☐ *The Runt Pig* book

Review

Review the Phonogram Cards that are behind the Review divider in your student's Reading Review Box. Show the card to your student and have him say the sound. If necessary, remind your student of the sound.

Review the Word Cards that are behind the Review divider in your student's Reading Review Box. If your student has difficulty reading the word, build the word with letter tiles and have your student sound it out using the procedure shown in Appendix C: Full Blending Procedure.

If your student has any difficulties in reading the next two stories, review the fluency sections of the previous lessons.

New Teaching

Read "The Big Mess"

"Do you like to cook and bake? What kinds of things do you like to make?" Discuss your student's experiences in the kitchen.

"The boy in this story likes to make pancakes. Let's see what happens. Turn to page 113."

Have your student read the story "The Big Mess."

Read "The Plan"

"Do you have a favorite blanket or pillow? Why do you like it so much?" Discuss where the student got the favorite item and why it's so special.

"The girl in this story gets a wonderful gift from her grandmother. Let's see what it is. Turn to page 125."

Have your student read the story "The Plan."

Read-Aloud Time   Read a Story or Poem

Read aloud to your student for twenty minutes.

Track Your Progress   Mark the Progress Chart

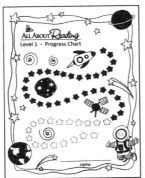

Have your student mark Lesson 31 on the Progress Chart.

Lesson 32 - Read "The Runt Pig"

In this lesson, your student will apply what he has learned by reading a story.

You will need: ☐ *The Runt Pig* book

Review

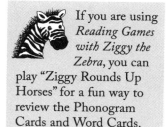

If you are using *Reading Games with Ziggy the Zebra*, you can play "Ziggy Rounds Up Horses" for a fun way to review the Phonogram Cards and Word Cards.

Review the Phonogram Cards that are behind the Review divider in your student's Reading Review Box. Show the card to your student and have him say the sound. If necessary, remind your student of the sound.

Review the Word Cards that are behind the Review divider in your student's Reading Review Box. If your student has difficulty reading the word, build the word with letter tiles and have your student sound it out using the procedure shown in Appendix C: Full Blending Procedure.

If your student has any difficulties in reading the next story, review the fluency sections of the previous lessons.

New Teaching

Read "The Runt Pig"

"Did a friend or relative ever need your help with something? How did you feel after you helped this person?" Discuss your student's experience.

"In the next story, a little pig is a big help to his fellow animals on the farm. Let's see what happens. Turn to page 135."

Have your student read the story "The Runt Pig."

Read-Aloud Time   Read a Story or Poem

Read aloud to your student for twenty minutes.

Track Your Progress

Mark the Progress Chart

Have your student mark Lesson 32 on the Progress Chart.

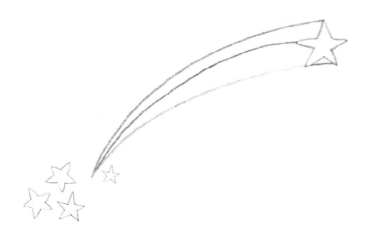

Lesson 32: Read "The Runt Pig"

Lesson 33 - Consonant Team <u>ck</u>

This lesson will teach words containing the consonant team <u>ck</u>.

You will need: ☐ Phonogram Card 30 ☐ *Blast Off to Reading!* pages 123-137
☐ Letter tile <u>ck</u> ☐ Word Cards 127-133

Before You Begin

Preview the Sounds of the Letters

Listen to the *Phonogram Sounds* app for a demonstration of the phonogram sound in today's lesson.

ck The consonant team <u>ck</u> says /k/ as in *duck*. It is typically found immediately after a short vowel.

Place the <u>ck</u> tile under the Consonant Teams label.

Review

Review the Phonogram Cards that are behind the Review divider in your student's Reading Review Box. Show the card to your student and have him say the sound. If necessary, remind your student of the sound.

Review the Word Cards that are behind the Review divider in your student's Reading Review Box. If your student has difficulty reading the word, build the word with letter tiles and have your student sound it out using the procedure shown in Appendix C: Full Blending Procedure.

New Teaching

Teach New Letter Sounds

"Point to the letter tiles that can say /k/." *Student points to the c and k tiles.*

"Today you will learn another letter tile that can say /k/." Set out the ck tile.

"The c and k work together to say one sound: /k/."

Teach the Phonogram Card for the consonant team ck.

1. Hold up the Phonogram Card and say the sound.
2. Have your student repeat the sound.

File the Phonogram Card behind the Review divider of the Reading Review Box.

Blend Sounds with Letter Tiles

Build the word *pick* with letter tiles. 　p　 i 　ck

"I'll sound out this first word, and then you'll sound out the next word."

Touch the p and say /p/.

Touch the i and say /ĭ/.

Touch the ck and say /k/.

New Teaching
(continued)

Now go back to the beginning of the word. Slide your finger under the letters p-i-ck and say *pick* slowly.

Finally, read the word *pick* at a normal pace, as we do when we speak.

Using the same procedure for blending, have your student sound out the word *neck*.

n	e	ck

Play "Change the Word"

Build the word *snack*.

s	n	a	ck

"What is this word?" *Snack.*

"I'm going to change the second letter of this word."

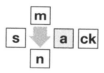

"What does this new word say?" Encourage your student to sound out the new word. *Smack.*

Continue to change one letter at a time to form the following words. Each time, have your student sound out the new word.

smack → sack → sick → pick → lick → luck → pluck

Return the letter tiles to their place in the alphabet.

New Teaching
(continued)

Complete Activity Sheets

Word Flipper

Remove pages 123-129 from the *Blast Off* activity book.

Each page will create one flipper. There are four Word Flippers in this lesson.

See the assembly instructions on page 125 of Lesson 22.

Have your student turn the pages and read the words that are formed.

A Flock of Ducks

Remove pages 131-133 from the *Blast Off* activity book.

Color the pond and ducks, if desired. Cut out the ducks.

Put the big ducks in one pile and the small ducks in another pile. Have your student turn one big duck over and read the word, then find the small duck that has the rhyming word. Put the pair in the pond.

Continue until all of the ducks are in the pond.

Practice Reading Words

Have your student practice reading the words on Word Cards 127-133.

stick — Level 1 – Lesson 33 Word Card 127

trick — Level 1 – Lesson 33 Word Card 128

check — Level 1 – Lesson 33 Word Card 129

clock — Level 1 – Lesson 33 Word Card 130

snack — Level 1 – Lesson 33 Word Card 131

neck — Level 1 – Lesson 33 Word Card 132

truck — Level 1 – Lesson 33 Word Card 133

File the Word Cards behind the Review divider of the Reading Review Box.

Lesson 33: Consonant Team <u>ck</u>

New Teaching
(continued)

Practice Fluency

Remove pages 135-137 from the *Blast Off* activity book.

Have your student read from the Fluency Practice sheets.

Read-Aloud Time

Read a Story or Poem

Read aloud to your student for twenty minutes.

Track Your Progress

Mark the Progress Chart

Have your student mark Lesson 33 on the Progress Chart.

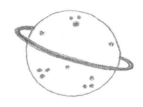

Lesson 34 - Read "Fun at the Pond" and "The Nap"

In this lesson, your student will apply what he has learned by reading two stories.

You will need: ☐ *Cobweb the Cat* book

Review

Review the Phonogram Cards that are behind the Review divider in your student's Reading Review Box. Show the card to your student and have him say the sound. If necessary, remind your student of the sound.

Review the Word Cards that are behind the Review divider in your student's Reading Review Box. If your student has difficulty reading the word, build the word with letter tiles and have your student sound it out using the procedure shown in Appendix C: Full Blending Procedure.

New Teaching

Read "Fun at the Pond"

"Do you know where frogs live? What other things could you see at a pond?" Possible answers include lily pads, cattails, fish, water, birds, sand, and butterflies.

"In the next story, three children have lots of fun at the pond. Let's see what they found there. Turn to page 9."

Have your student read the story "Fun at the Pond."

New Teaching
(continued)

Read "The Nap"

"Pretend you are a baby bear and you are very tired. What would be your favorite place to take a nap?" Discuss your student's ideas.

"Let's see what happens when the bear cub in this story takes a nap. Turn to page 29."

Have your student read the story "The Nap."

Read-Aloud Time

Read a Story or Poem

Read aloud to your student for twenty minutes.

Track Your Progress

Mark the Progress Chart

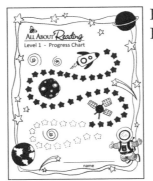

Have your student mark Lesson 34 on the Progress Chart.

Lesson 35 - Read "At Camp" and "The Pet Duck"

In this lesson, your student will apply what he has learned by reading two stories.

You will need: ☐ *Cobweb the Cat* book

Review

Review the Phonogram Cards that are behind the Review divider in your student's Reading Review Box. Show the card to your student and have him say the sound. If necessary, remind your student of the sound.

Review the Word Cards that are behind the Review divider in your student's Reading Review Box. If your student has difficulty reading the word, build the word with letter tiles and have your student sound it out using the procedure shown in Appendix C: Full Blending Procedure.

New Teaching

Read "At Camp"

"Have you ever been camping? What are some things you could do at a campsite?" Possible answers include set up a tent, build a campfire, go fishing, collect leaves, watch the animals, and roll out the sleeping bags.

"The two boys in this story go camping on the top of a hill. Turn to page 43."

Have your student read the story "At Camp."

New Teaching
(continued)

Read "The Pet Duck"

"Do you have any pets? What kinds of animals make the best pets? What kinds of trouble can pets get into?" Discuss your student's ideas.

"The little girl in the next story has a pet duck who gets into all sorts of trouble! Let's see what this duck does. Turn to page 57."

Have your student read the story "The Pet Duck."

Read-Aloud Time

Read a Story or Poem

Read aloud to your student for twenty minutes.

Track Your Progress

Mark the Progress Chart

Have your student mark Lesson 35 on the Progress Chart.

Lesson 36 - Consonant Team ng

This lesson will teach words containing the consonant team ng.

You will need:
- [ ] Phonogram Card 31
- [ ] Letter tile ng
- [ ] *Blast Off to Reading!* pages 139-143
- [ ] Word Cards 134-139

Before You Begin

Preview the Sounds of the Letters

Listen to the *Phonogram Sounds* app for a demonstration of the phonogram sound in today's lesson.

ng The consonant team ng says /ng/ as in *ring*.

Place the ng tile under the Consonant Teams label.

Review

Review the Phonogram Cards that are behind the Review divider in your student's Reading Review Box. Show the card to your student and have him say the sound. If necessary, remind your student of the sound.

Review the Word Cards that are behind the Review divider in your student's Reading Review Box. If your student has difficulty reading the word, build the word with letter tiles and have your student sound it out using the procedure shown in Appendix C: Full Blending Procedure.

New Teaching

Teach New Letter Sounds

Teach the Phonogram Card for the consonant team <u>ng</u>.

ng

Level 1 – Lesson 36   Phonogram Card 31

1. Hold up the Phonogram Card and say the sound.
2. Have your student repeat the sound.

Set out the new letter tile. Practice with the letter tile until your student can say the sound accurately. **ng**

Blend Sounds with Letter Tiles

Build the word part *ang* with letter tiles. **a** **ng**

"This word part says /ang/. Let's make some words with /ang/."

One at a time, build the words *bang, fang, hang,* and *rang*, and read them with your student.

b **a** **ng**   **f** **a** **ng**   **h** **a** **ng**   **r** **a** **ng**

Build the word part *ing* with letter tiles. **i** **ng**

"This word part says /ing/."

Build the words *sing, king, ring, thing,* and *wing*, and read them with your student.

s **i** **ng**   **k** **i** **ng**   **r** **i** **ng**   **th** **i** **ng**   **w** **i** **ng**

Build the word part *ong*. **o** **ng**

"<u>Ng</u> can be combined with <u>o</u>, too. The <u>o</u> says /ŏ/ just like we expect it to say."

Build the words *song, long,* and *gong*, and read them with your student.

s **o** **ng**   **l** **o** **ng**   **g** **o** **ng**

When phonogram <u>ng</u> comes after <u>a</u> and <u>i</u>, the vowels don't say their pure short vowel sound. Instead, the sound falls between the short and long vowel sound, as in the words *sang* and *thing*.

This concept is generally easy for students to grasp, since it is difficult to say the pure short vowel sound in these word parts. It is easier to say the word parts correctly.

Less commonly, <u>ng</u> combines with <u>e</u> to form the word part *eng*, as in *English* and *strength*. There are only a few words with the *eng* word part, and since none of them appear at this reading level, words containing *eng* have not been included in this exercise.

Lesson 36: Consonant Team <u>ng</u>

New Teaching
(continued)

Build the word part *ung*.

"And n̲g̲ can be combined with u̲. The u̲ says /ŭ/ just like we expect it to say."

Build the words *hung*, *sung*, *flung*, and *lung*, and read them with your student.

| h | u | ng | | s | u | ng | | f | l | u | ng | | l | u | ng |

Arrange the letter tiles like this:

Point to the *ang* word part. "Say this word part." *Ang.*

Move the n̲g̲ down to form the *ing* word part. "Say this word part." *Ing.*

Repeat with the remaining vowels, and then do mixed review until your student can easily read all four word parts.

Play "Change the Word"

Build the word *thing*. th i ng

"What is this word?" *Thing.*

"I'm going to change the first letter of this word."

"What does this new word say?" Encourage your student to sound out the new word. *Ring.*

Continue to change one letter at a time to form the following words. Each time, have your student sound out the new word.

ring → rang → sang → sing → song → sung → stung → sting

Return the letter tiles to their place in the alphabet.

New Teaching

Complete Activity Sheet

Matching Mittens

Remove pages 139-140 from the *Blast Off* activity book.

Cut out the kitten and all of the mittens.

Lay the mittens on a table with the words facing down and mix them up.

Have your student choose a pair of matching mittens, flip them over to read the rhyming words, and then place the matching mittens on the kitten's paws.

Repeat until the kitten has tried on all the mittens.

Practice Reading Words

Have your student practice reading the words on Word Cards 134-139.

File the Word Cards behind the Review divider of the Reading Review Box.

New Teaching
(continued)

Practice Fluency

Remove pages 141-143 from the *Blast Off* activity book.

Have your student read from the Fluency Practice sheets.

Read-Aloud Time

Read a Story or Poem

Read aloud to your student for twenty minutes.

Track Your Progress

Mark the Progress Chart

Have your student mark Lesson 36 on the Progress Chart.

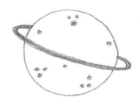

Lesson 37 - Read "The Bat and King Sam"

In this lesson, your student will apply what he has learned by reading a story.

You will need: ☐ *Cobweb the Cat* book

Review

Review the Phonogram Cards that are behind the Review divider in your student's Reading Review Box. Show the card to your student and have him say the sound. If necessary, remind your student of the sound.

Review the Word Cards that are behind the Review divider in your student's Reading Review Box. If your student has difficulty reading the word, build the word with letter tiles and have your student sound it out using the procedure shown in Appendix C: Full Blending Procedure.

Shuffle the cards behind the **Mastered** dividers and choose a selection for review.

New Teaching

Read "The Bat and King Sam"

"Do you like to sing songs? What song makes you feel happy and cheerful?" Discuss the student's favorite songs to sing.

"In this next story, a very special animal sings songs to cheer up a new friend. Let's see what happens. Turn to page 73."

Have your student read the story "The Bat and King Sam."

Read-Aloud Time

Read a Story or Poem

Read aloud to your student for twenty minutes.

Track Your Progress

Mark the Progress Chart

Have your student mark Lesson 37 on the Progress Chart.

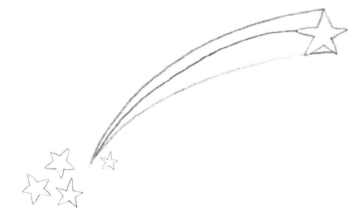

Lesson 37: Read "The Bat and King Sam"

Lesson 38 - Consonant Team <u>nk</u>

This lesson will teach words containing the consonant team <u>nk</u>.

You will need: ☐ Phonogram Card 32   ☐ *Blast Off to Reading!* pages 145-151

☐ Letter tile <u>nk</u>   ☐ Word Cards 140-146

Before You Begin

Preview the Sounds of the Letters

Listen to the *Phonogram Sounds* app for a demonstration of the phonogram sound in today's lesson.

<u>nk</u> The consonant team <u>nk</u> says /ngk/ as in *think*.

Place the <u>nk</u> tile under the Consonant Teams label.

Review

Review the Phonogram Cards that are behind the Review divider in your student's Reading Review Box. Show the card to your student and have him say the sound. If necessary, remind your student of the sound.

Review the Word Cards that are behind the Review divider in your student's Reading Review Box. If your student has difficulty reading the word, build the word with letter tiles and have your student sound it out using the procedure shown in Appendix C: Full Blending Procedure.

New Teaching

Teach New Letter Sounds

Teach the Phonogram Card for the consonant team <u>nk</u>.

Level 1 – Lesson 38   Phonogram Card 32

1. Hold up the Phonogram Card and say the sound.
2. Have your student repeat the sound.

Set out the new letter tile. Practice with the letter tile until your student can say the sound accurately. `nk`

Blend Sounds with Letter Tiles

> Consonant team <u>nk</u> influences the vowels <u>a</u> and <u>i</u>, just as <u>ng</u> does. The vowels don't say their pure short vowel sound. Instead, the sound falls between the short and long vowel sound, as in the words *rank* and *think*.
>
> This concept is generally easy for students to grasp, since it is difficult to say the pure short vowel sound in these word parts. It is easier to say the word parts correctly.
>
> It is interesting to note that <u>nk</u> never combines with <u>e</u> to form words. There is no word part *enk*.

Arrange the letter tiles like this:

`a` `nk`
`i`
`o`
`u`

Point to the *ank* word part. "This word part says /ank/. Say this word part." *Ank.*

Move the <u>nk</u> down to form the *ink* word part. "This word part says /ink/. Say this word part." *Ink.*

Repeat with word parts *onk* and *unk*, and then do mixed review until your student can easily read all four word parts.

"Let's make some words with *ank*." One at a time, build the words *bank, sank,* and *thank,* and read them with your student.

`b` `a` `nk`   `s` `a` `nk`   `th` `a` `nk`

"Let's make some words with *ink*." One at a time, build the words *think, clink,* and *drink,* and read them with your student.

`th` `i` `nk`   `c` `l` `i` `nk`   `d` `r` `i` `nk`

New Teaching
(continued)

"Let's make some words with *onk*." Build the words *honk* and *bonk* and read them with your student.

"Let's make some words with *unk*." Build the words *hunk*, *bunk*, and *sunk* and read them with your student.

h | u | nk   b | u | nk   s | u | nk

Play "Change the Word"

Build the word *pink*.   p | i | nk

"What is this word?" *Pink.*

"I'm going to change the first letter of this word."

"What does this new word say?" Encourage your student to sound out the new word. *Rink.*

Continue to change the letters to form the following words. Each time, have your student sound out the new word.

> rink → shrink → shrunk
>
> sunk → junk → bunk → bank → thank → think → ink

Return the letter tiles to their place in the alphabet.

Complete Activity Sheet

<u>**Word Flipper**</u>
Remove pages 145-147 from the *Blast Off* activity book.

Each page will create one flipper. There are two Word Flippers in this lesson.

See the assembly instructions on page 125 of Lesson 22.

Have your student turn the pages and read the words that are formed.

Practice Reading Words

Have your student practice reading the words on Word Cards 140-146.

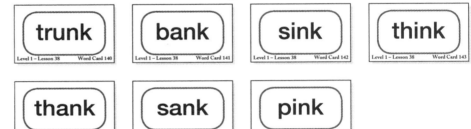

File the Word Cards behind the Review divider of the Reading Review Box.

Practice Fluency

Remove pages 149-151 from the *Blast Off* activity book.

Have your student read from the Fluency Practice sheet.

Read-Aloud Time   Read a Story or Poem

Read aloud to your student for twenty minutes.

Track Your Progress

Mark the Progress Chart

Have your student mark Lesson 38 on the Progress Chart.

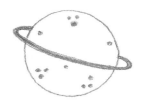

Lesson 39 - Read "Frank Shrank!"

In this lesson, your student will apply what he has learned by reading a story.

You will need: ☐ *Cobweb the Cat* book

Review

Review the Phonogram Cards that are behind the Review divider in your student's Reading Review Box. Show the card to your student and have him say the sound. If necessary, remind your student of the sound.

Review the Word Cards that are behind the Review divider in your student's Reading Review Box. If your student has difficulty reading the word, build the word with letter tiles and have your student sound it out using the procedure shown in Appendix C: Full Blending Procedure.

New Teaching

Read "Frank Shrank!"

"Pretend that you are only two inches tall. Where do you think you would sleep at night? How would you travel from place to place?" Ask the student how he might use various common objects, such as a teacup, a sponge, a ruler, a straw.

"The boy in this story is very small. Let's see what kind of adventures he has. Turn to page 83."

Have your student read the story "Frank Shrank!"

Read-Aloud Time

Read a Story or Poem

Read aloud to your student for twenty minutes.

Track Your Progress

Mark the Progress Chart

Have your student mark Lesson 39 on the Progress Chart.

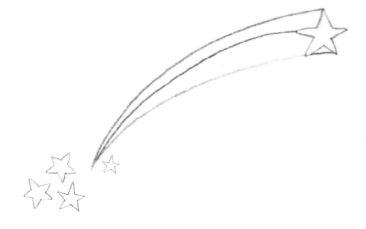

Lesson 39: Read "Frank Shrank!"

Lesson 40 - Compound Words

This lesson will teach compound words, as well as the sight word <u>do</u>.

You will need: ☐ *Blast Off to Reading!* pages 153-164

☐ *Word Cards 147-157*

Before You Begin

Add Letter Tiles to the Magnetic White Board

In today's lesson, your student will begin building compound words, which require more letters. Add the remaining tiles from the second set of <u>a</u>-<u>z</u> letter tiles to complete your setup.

Review

Review the Phonogram Cards that are behind the Review divider in your student's Reading Review Box. Show the card to your student and have him say the sound. If necessary, remind your student of the sound.

Review the Word Cards that are behind the Review divider in your student's Reading Review Box. If your student has difficulty reading the word, build the word with letter tiles and have your student sound it out using the procedure shown in Appendix C: Full Blending Procedure.

New Teaching

Teach Compound Words

Build the word *bathtub* with letter tiles. b a th t u b

"The word *bathtub* has two smaller words in it. Can you find the two smaller words?" *Bath, tub.*

"Good! Two smaller words put together form a special type of word. We call this type of word a *compound word.*"

Complete Activity Sheets

Bird Friends

Remove pages 153-155 from the *Blast Off* activity book.

Cut out the branch and the birds. Lay the birds on the table and mix them up. Your child should select two matching birds, set them on the branch side by side, and read the resulting compound word.

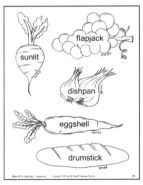

Chop-Chop

Remove pages 157-159 from the *Blast Off* activity book.

Cut out the knife and the foods.

Have your student pretend to cut each compound word between its two smaller words. He should then read each smaller word, and then the compound word.

Practice Reading Words

Have your student practice reading the words on Word Cards 147-156.

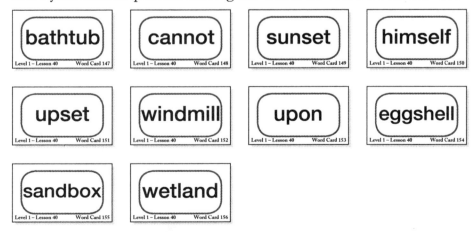

File the Word Cards behind the Review divider of the Reading Review Box.

Lesson 40: Compound Words

Teach a Sight Word: *do*

"Today we have another word that doesn't say what we expect it to say."

Show Word Card 157 to your student.

"This word is *do*, as in *What did you do today?*"

Review this word several times today and then file it behind the Review divider.

We are treating the word *do* as a sight word because it contains the third sound of <u>o</u>, which has not been taught yet.

Practice Fluency

Remove pages 161-164 from the *Blast Off* activity book.

Have your student read from the Fluency Practice sheets.

Read-Aloud Time   Read a Story or Poem

Read aloud to your student for twenty minutes.

Track Your Progress

Mark the Progress Chart

Have your student mark Lesson 40 on the Progress Chart.

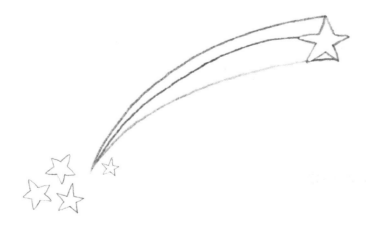

Lesson 41 - Read "Cobweb the Cat"

In this lesson, your student will apply what he has learned by reading a story.

You will need: ☐ *Cobweb the Cat* book

Review

Review the Phonogram Cards that are behind the Review divider in your student's Reading Review Box. Show the card to your student and have him say the sound. If necessary, remind your student of the sound.

Review the Word Cards that are behind the Review divider in your student's Reading Review Box. If your student has difficulty reading the word, build the word with letter tiles and have your student sound it out using the procedure shown in Appendix C: Full Blending Procedure.

New Teaching

Read "Cobweb the Cat"

"Do you or does someone you know have a pet cat? What do you think cats like to do for fun? Where do they like to go?" Discuss your student's ideas.

"The cat in this story is very busy. Let's see what he does all day. Turn to page 99."

Have your student read the story "Cobweb the Cat."

Read-Aloud Time

Read a Story or Poem

Read aloud to your student for twenty minutes.

Track Your Progress

Mark the Progress Chart

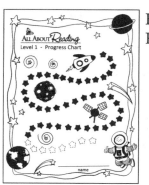

Have your student mark Lesson 41 on the Progress Chart.

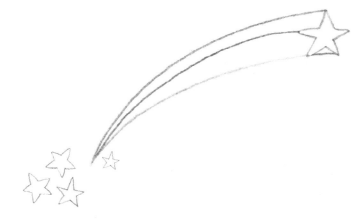

Lesson 42 - Plural Words

This lesson will teach plural words.

You will need: ☐ *Blast Off to Reading!* pages 165-170

☐ Word Cards 158-167

Before You Begin

Add a Letter Tile to the Magnetic White Board

In today's lesson, your student will begin building plural words. Add the third s̲ tile to your letter tile setup.

Review

Phonogram Cards

Review the Phonogram Cards that are behind the Review divider in your student's Reading Review Box. Show the card to your student and have him say the sound. If necessary, remind your student of the sound.

Word Cards

Review the Word Cards that are behind the Review divider in your student's Reading Review Box. If your student has difficulty reading the word, build the word with letter tiles and have your student sound it out using the procedure shown in Appendix C: Full Blending Procedure.

New Teaching

The letter s̲ says /z/ after vowel sounds (as in *plays*) and after voiced consonants (as in *bugs*). With a bit of experience, your student will automatically choose the correct pronunciation of the letter s̲ without giving it any conscious thought. It is actually more difficult to say the incorrect pronunciation for the letter s̲.

Teach Plural Words

Build the word *hats* with the tiles. 　h a t s

Cover the s̲ with your finger.

"We say one *hat*..."　　

"...and we say two *hats*."　　

"*Hats* is **plural** because it means **more than one**."

New Teaching
(continued)

"I'll say a word and you make it plural."

"One *map*, two _____." If necessary, prompt your student to say *maps*.

"One *ant*, two _____. *Ants.*

"One *star*, two _____. *Stars.*

"At the end of a word, the <u>s</u> can say either /s/ or /z/. First try the /s/ sound, and if that doesn't sound right, try the /z/ sound."

Build the following words and have your student read them.

| c | u | p | s | | b | u | g | s | | t | e | n | t | s |

Build the word *glasses* with the tiles. | g | l | a | s | s | e | s |

> The suffix *es* is found after the sounds /s/, /z/, /ch/, /sh/, and /ks/.

Cover the <u>e</u>-<u>s</u> with your finger.

"We say one *glass*..." | g | l | a | s | s |

"...and we say two *glasses*." | g | l | a | s | s | e | s |

"*Glasses* is **plural** because it means **more than one**."

Build the following words and have your student read them.

| d | i | sh | e | s | | k | i | s | s | e | s | | b | o | x | e | s |

Complete Activity Sheet

<u>Have a Ball</u>
Remove pages 165-166 from the *Blast Off* activity book.

Cut out the twelve sports items. Place the six balls in one group with the words facing down. Mix them up.

Place the six items of sports equipment in another group, with the words facing down.

Have your student match each ball with the corresponding piece of sports equipment. He should then flip them over and read the singular and plural versions of the words.

Lesson 42: Plural Words

Practice Reading Words

Have your student practice reading the words on Word Cards 158-167.

File the Word Cards behind the Review divider of the Reading Review Box.

Practice Fluency

Remove pages 167-170 from the *Blast Off* activity book.

Have your student read from the Fluency Practice sheets.

Read-Aloud Time   Read a Story or Poem

Read aloud to your student for twenty minutes.

Track Your Progress

Mark the Progress Chart

Have your student mark Lesson 42 on the Progress Chart.

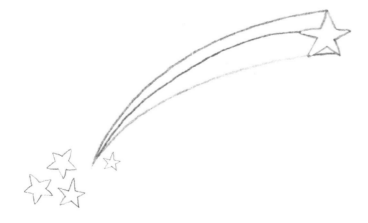

Lesson 42: Plural Words

Lesson 43 - Read "Ten Wishes" and "Fast Fun"

In this lesson, your student will apply what he has learned by reading a story and learning some tongue twisters.

You will need: ☐ *Cobweb the Cat* book

Review

Review the Phonogram Cards that are behind the Review divider in your student's Reading Review Box. Show the card to your student and have him say the sound. If necessary, remind your student of the sound.

Review the Word Cards that are behind the Review divider in your student's Reading Review Box. If your student has difficulty reading the word, build the word with letter tiles and have your student sound it out using the procedure shown in Appendix C: Full Blending Procedure.

New Teaching

Read "Ten Wishes"

"Suppose that for one day, you were allowed to have the one thing you want most in the world. What would you ask for?" Discuss your student's ideas.

"Let's see what the children in this story would ask for. Turn to page 115."

Have your student read the story "Ten Wishes."

Read "Fast Fun"

"Do you know what a tongue twister is? It's a silly sentence that's hard to say, like *Red baby buggy bumpers*. Let's see if you can say the tongue twisters in the next story. Turn to page 131."

Have your student read "Fast Fun."

Read-Aloud Time   Read a Story or Poem

Read aloud to your student for twenty minutes.

Track Your Progress

Mark the Progress Chart

Have your student mark Lesson 43 on the Progress Chart.

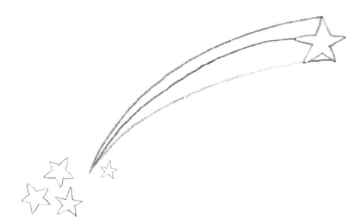

Lesson 44 - Additional Sounds for <u>a</u>, <u>i</u>, and <u>c</u>

This lesson will teach additional sounds for the letters <u>a</u>, <u>i</u>, and <u>c</u>.

You will need:
- [ ] Phonogram Cards 4, 11, and 16
- [ ] Letter tiles <u>a</u>, <u>i</u>, and <u>c</u>
- [ ] *Blast Off to Reading!* page 171

Before You Begin

Preview the Sounds of the Letters

 Listen to the *Phonogram Sounds* app for a reminder of the phonogram sounds in today's lesson.

Review

 Review the Phonogram Cards that are behind the Review divider in your student's Reading Review Box. Show the card to your student and have him say the sound. If necessary, remind your student of the sound.

 Review the Word Cards that are behind the Review divider in your student's Reading Review Box. If your student has difficulty reading the word, build the word with letter tiles and have your student sound it out using the procedure shown in Appendix C: Full Blending Procedure.

New Teaching

In future lessons, your student will learn when each of these letters can say their first, second, and third sounds.

Teach New Letter Sounds

 Take out Phonogram Card 4 and show it to your student.

"You already know that the letter <u>a</u> says /ă/. But it also makes two other sounds: /ā/ and /ah/. So the letter <u>a</u> makes three sounds: /ă/, /ā/, and /ah/. Repeat after me: /ă/–/ā/–/ah/." *Student repeats.*

New Teaching
(continued)

Take out Phonogram Card 16 and show it to your student.

"You already know that the letter i̲ says /ĭ/. But it also makes two other sounds: /ī/ and /ē/. So the letter i̲ makes three sounds: /ĭ/, /ī/, and /ē/. Repeat after me: /ĭ/–/ī/–/ē/." *Student repeats.*

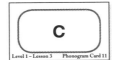

Take out Phonogram Card 11 and show it to your student.

"You already know that the letter c̲ says /k/. But it also makes another sound, /s/. So the letter c̲ makes two sounds: /k/ and /s/. Repeat after me: /k/–/s/." *Student repeats.*

Set out the letter tiles and practice until your student can say the sounds accurately.

`a` `i` `c`

If you are using *Reading Games with Ziggy the Zebra*, you can play "Ziggy Plays with Penguins" for an engaging way to practice the Phonogram Cards.

Complete Activity Sheet

Load the Train
Remove page 171 from the *Blast Off* activity book.

Give your student something fun to use for markers, like raisins, M&Ms, coins, jelly beans, or Cheerios.

Randomly call out the sounds of the letters. For instance, for the letter i̲, ask your student to place a jelly bean over the letter that can say /ĭ/–/ī/–/ē/. As you call each sound or group of sounds, your student should put a marker over the corresponding letter. When the student has filled all eight parts of the train, he says "Choo-choo!"

Lesson 44: Additional Sounds for a̲, i̲, and c̲

Read-Aloud Time   Read a Story or Poem

Read aloud to your student for twenty minutes.

Track Your Progress

Mark the Progress Chart

Have your student mark Lesson 44 on the Progress Chart.

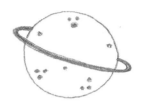

Lesson 45 - Additional Sounds for <u>o</u> and <u>g</u>

This lesson will teach additional sounds for the letters <u>o</u> and <u>g</u>.

You will need: ☐ Phonogram Cards 9 and 20

☐ Letter tiles <u>o</u> and <u>g</u>

☐ *Blast Off to Reading!* page 173

Before You Begin

Preview the Sounds of the Letters

Listen to the *Phonogram Sounds* app for a reminder of the phonogram sounds in today's lesson.

Review

Review the Phonogram Cards that are behind the Review divider in your student's Reading Card Box. Show the card to your student and have him say the sound. If necessary, remind your student of the sound.

Review the Word Cards that are behind the Review divider in your student's Reading Card Box. If your student has difficulty reading the word, build the word with letter tiles and have your student sound it out using the procedure shown in Appendix C: Full Blending Procedure.

New Teaching

Teach New Letter Sounds

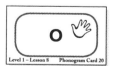

Take out Phonogram Card 20 and show it to your student.

"You already know that the letter <u>o</u> says /ŏ/. But it also makes three other sounds: /ō/, /o͞o/, and /ŭ/. So the letter <u>o</u> makes four sounds: /ŏ/, /ō/, /o͞o/, and /ŭ/. Repeat after me: /ŏ/–/ō/–/o͞o/–/ŭ/." *Student repeats.*

New Teaching
(continued)

Level 1 - Lesson 3   Phonogram Card 9

Take out Phonogram Card 9 and show it to your student.

"You already know that the letter g says /g/. But it also makes another sound, /j/. So the letter g makes two sounds: /g/ and /j/. Repeat after me: /g/–/j/." *Student repeats.*

Set out the letter tiles and practice until your student can say the sounds accurately.

[o] [g]

Complete Activity Sheet

Ride 'em, Cowboy!
Remove page 173 from the *Blast Off* activity book.

Give your student something fun to use for markers, like raisins, M&Ms, coins, jelly beans, or Cheerios.

Randomly call out the sounds of the letters. For instance, for the letter g, ask your student to place a jelly bean over the letter that can say /g/–/j/. As you call each sound or group of sounds, your student should put a marker over the corresponding letter. When the student has filled all six saddles, he says "Ride 'em Cowboy!"

Read-Aloud Time   Read a Story or Poem

Read aloud to your student for twenty minutes.

Lesson 45: Additional Sounds for o and g

Track Your Progress

Mark the Progress Chart

Have your student mark Lesson 45 on the Progress Chart.

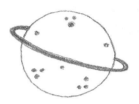

Lesson 46 - Additional Sounds for <u>e</u>, <u>u</u>, <u>y</u>, and <u>ch</u>

This lesson will teach additional sounds for the letters <u>e</u>, <u>u</u>, <u>y</u>, and <u>ch</u>.

You will need: ☐ Phonogram Cards 12, 23, 24, 29

☐ Letter tiles <u>e</u>, <u>u</u>, red <u>y</u>, and <u>ch</u>

☐ *Blast Off to Reading!* page 175

Before You Begin

Preview the Sounds of the Letters

Listen to the *Phonogram Sounds* app for a reminder of the phonogram sounds in today's lesson.

Review

Review the Phonogram Cards that are behind the Review divider in your student's Reading Review Box. Show the card to your student and have him say the sound. If necessary, remind your student of the sound.

Review the Word Cards that are behind the Review divider in your student's Reading Review Box. If your student has difficulty reading the word, build the word with letter tiles and have your student sound it out using the procedure shown in Appendix C: Full Blending Procedure.

Shuffle the cards behind the **Mastered** dividers and choose a selection for review.

New Teaching

Teach New Letter Sounds

Take out Phonogram Card 24 and show it to your student.

"You already know that the letter e says /ĕ/. But it also makes another sound: /ē/. So the letter e makes two sounds: /ĕ/ and /ē/. Repeat after me: /ĕ/–/ē/." *Student repeats.*

Take out Phonogram Card 23 and show it to your student.

"You already know that the letter u says /ŭ/. But it also makes two other sounds: /ū/ and /o͞o/. So the letter u makes three sounds: /ŭ/, /ū/, and /o͞o/. Repeat after me: /ŭ/–/ū/–/o͞o/." *Student repeats.*

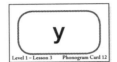

Take out Phonogram Card 12 and show it to your student.

"You already know that the letter y says /y/. But it also makes three other sounds: /ĭ/, /ī/, and /ē/. So the letter y makes four sounds: /y/, /ĭ/, /ī/, and /ē/. Repeat after me: /y/–/ĭ/–/ī/–/ē/." *Student repeats.*

Take out Phonogram Card 29 and show it to your student.

"You already know that consonant team ch says /ch/. But it also makes two other sounds: /k/ and /sh/. So consonant team ch makes three sounds: /ch/, /k/, and /sh/. Repeat after me: /ch/–/k/–/sh/." *Student repeats.*

Set out the letter tiles and practice until your student can say the sounds accurately.

Lesson 46: Additional Sounds for e, u, y, and ch

New Teaching
(continued)

Complete Activity Sheet

Dump Trucks

Remove page 175 from the *Blast Off* activity book.

Give your student something fun to use for markers, like raisins, M&Ms, coins, jelly beans, or Cheerios.

Randomly call out the sounds of the letters. For instance, for the letter y, ask your student to place a jelly bean over the letter that can say /y/–/ĭ/–/ī/–/ē/. As you call each sound or group of sounds, your student should put a marker over the corresponding letter. When the student has filled all six of the trucks, he says "Dump it!"

Read-Aloud Time

Read a Story or Poem

Read aloud to your student for twenty minutes.

Track Your Progress

Mark the Progress Chart

Have your student mark Lesson 46 on the Progress Chart.

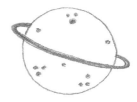

Lesson 47 - Short Vowels and Counting Syllables

This lesson will teach the term *short vowel sounds* and how to count syllables.

You will need: ☐ letter tiles <u>a</u>, <u>e</u>, <u>i</u>, <u>o</u>, and <u>u</u>

☐ *Blast Off to Reading!* pages 177-180

Review

Review the Phonogram Cards that are behind the Review divider in your student's Reading Review Box. Show the card to your student and have him say the sound. If necessary, remind your student of the sound.

Review the Word Cards that are behind the Review divider in your student's Reading Review Box. If your student has difficulty reading the word, build the word with letter tiles and have your student sound it out using the procedure shown in Appendix C: Full Blending Procedure.

New Teaching

Teach Short Vowel Sounds

Put the letter tiles <u>a</u>, <u>e</u>, <u>i</u>, <u>o</u>, and <u>u</u> in front of the student.

Point to the <u>a</u> tile.

"Tell me the three sounds of this letter." /ă/–/ā/–/ah/.

"Which of those sounds is the **short** sound?" /ă/ (or *the first sound*).

"Good. The first sound you said, /ă/, is called the **short sound of <u>a</u>**."

Point to the <u>e</u> tile.

"What sounds does this letter make?" /ĕ/–/ē/.

"Good. The first sound you said, /ĕ/, is called the **short sound of <u>e</u>**."

Repeat this activity with letter tiles <u>i</u>, <u>o</u>, and <u>u</u> so the student can see that the first sound is the short sound.

> In the next lesson, your student will learn the term for the second sound of a vowel: the long vowel sound.

New Teaching
(continued)

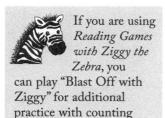

If you are using *Reading Games with Ziggy the Zebra*, you can play "Blast Off with Ziggy" for additional practice with counting syllables.

Counting Syllables

In this next exercise, you will demonstrate what a syllable is by clapping your hands as you say the syllables.

"All words have syllables. A word might have one, two, or even more syllables."

"*Swimming* has two syllables: *swim* [clap] *–ing* [clap]."
"*Grass* has one syllable: *grass* [clap]."
"*Reindeer* has two syllables: *rein* [clap] *–deer* [clap]."

"Now you try. Clap your hands for each syllable in the word *dog*."

Have your student practice with these words:

ham	**telephone**	**sixteen**	**grape**	**table**
butterfly	**ring**	**zipper**	**tent**	**purple**

Here are two more methods for teaching how to count syllables:

1. Have the student put his hand under his chin, say the word, and count how many times his jaw drops.

2. Have younger students jump for each "chunk" of the word. Each jump represents one syllable.

Complete Activity Sheet

Cute Critters
Remove pages 177-180 from the *Blast Off* activity book.

Cut out all the cards. Mix them up and lay them on the table.

Lay out the numbers 1, 2, and 3, which represent possible numbers of syllables. Have your student sort the cards into three piles according to the number of syllables in the animals' names.

Lesson 47: Short Vowels and Counting Syllables

Read-Aloud Time   Read a Story or Poem

Read aloud to your student for twenty minutes.

Track Your Progress

Mark the Progress Chart

Have your student mark Lesson 47 on the Progress Chart.

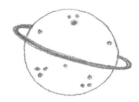

Lesson 48 - Open and Closed Syllables

This lesson will teach long vowel sounds and words containing open syllables.

You will need: ☐ letter tiles <u>a</u>, <u>e</u>, <u>i</u>, <u>o</u>, and <u>u</u>   ☐ Word Cards 168-174

☐ *Blast Off to Reading!* pages 181-189

Review

Review the Phonogram Cards that are behind the Review divider in your student's Reading Review Box. Show the card to your student and have him say the sound. If necessary, remind your student of the sound.

Review the Word Cards that are behind the Review divider in your student's Reading Review Box. If your student has difficulty reading the word, build the word with letter tiles and have your student sound it out using the procedure shown in Appendix C: Full Blending Procedure.

One at a time, point to the letter tiles <u>a</u>, <u>e</u>, <u>i</u>, <u>o</u>, and <u>u</u>. Have your student tell you the short vowel sound of each letter.

New Teaching

Teach Long Vowel Sounds

Put the letter tiles <u>a</u>, <u>e</u>, <u>i</u>, <u>o</u>, and <u>u</u> in front of the student.

Point to the <u>a</u> tile.   <kbd>a</kbd>

"Tell me the three sounds of this letter." /ă/–/ā/–/ah/.

"Which of those sounds is the **short** sound?" /ă/ (or *the first sound*).

"Good. The first sound of a vowel is its short sound. We also have a name for the **second** sound of a vowel. The second sound is called its **long** sound."

"What is the second sound of the letter <u>a</u>?" /ā/.

New Teaching
(continued)

Point to the e tile. `e`

"What are the two sounds of this letter?" /ĕ/–/ē/.

"What is the long sound of this letter?" /ē/.

Point to the i tile. `i`

"What are the three sounds of this letter?" /ĭ/–/ī/–/ē/.

"What is the long sound of this letter?" /ī/.

Point to the o tile. `o`

Your student can probably see the pattern now.

"And what do you think the long sound of o is?" /ō/.

"And the long sound of u is?" /ū/. `u`

"Good. The long sound of a letter is the same as its name."

Teach Closed and Open Syllables

Build the word *shed*. `sh` `e` `d`

"Point to the vowel." *Student points to the e.*

"Is there anything after the e?" *Yes, d.*

"Good. We say that the e is closed in by the d. This is a **closed** syllable."

"Is the vowel in this word short or long?" *Short.*

"Right. When a vowel is in a **closed** syllable, it usually says its **short** sound."

"What is this word?" *Shed.*

Remove the d tile. `sh` `e`

"Is there anything after the e now?" *No.*

"We can say that the e is **open**, because there is nothing closing it in."

Lesson 48: Open and Closed Syllables

New Teaching
(continued)

"When a vowel is in an **open** syllable, it usually says its **long** sound."

Point to the <u>e</u>. "What does the <u>e</u> say in this word?" /ē/.

"This word says…?" *She.*

Build the following words. Have your student tell you whether the syllable is **open** or **closed**.

he	*Open.*
hem	*Closed.*
so	*Open.*
sock	*Closed.*
got	*Closed.*

For additional practice, use the following words:

go	**wet**	**we**	**no**	**not**
I	**it**	**bed**	**be**	

Practice Reading Words

Have your student practice reading the words on Word Cards 168-174.

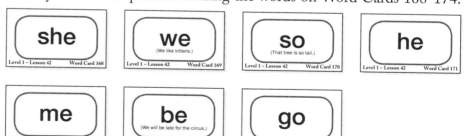

File the Word Cards behind the Review divider of the Reading Review Box.

Complete Activity Sheet

Space Ships

Remove pages 181-185 from the *Blast Off* activity book.

Color the spaceships and the astronauts, if desired. Cut out ships and astronauts.

Place the nine astronauts in a group with the words facing down and mix them up.

Have the student select an astronaut, read the word aloud, and then decide whether the syllable is open or closed. If the syllable is open, he can place the astronaut on the spaceship with the open door. If the syllable is closed, the astronaut can be placed on the spaceship with the closed door. Repeat until all of the astronauts are correctly placed.

Practice Fluency

Remove pages 187-189 from the *Blast Off* activity book.

Have your student read from the Fluency Practice sheets.

Read-Aloud Time   Read a Story or Poem

Read aloud to your student for twenty minutes.

Track Your Progress

Mark the Progress Chart

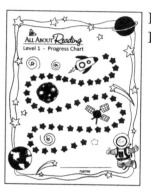

Have your student mark Lesson 48 on the Progress Chart.

Lesson 49 - Read "Off We Go!"

In this lesson, your student will apply what he has learned by reading a story.

You will need: ☐ *Cobweb the Cat* book

☐ *Certificate of Achievement*

Review

Review the Phonogram Cards that are behind the Review divider in your student's Reading Review Box. Show the card to your student and have him say the sound. If necessary, remind your student of the sound.

Review the Word Cards that are behind the Review divider in your student's Reading Review Box. If your student has difficulty reading the word, build the word with letter tiles and have your student sound it out using the procedure shown in Appendix C: Full Blending Procedure.

Review short and long vowels. One at a time, point to the letter tiles <u>a</u>, <u>e</u>, <u>i</u>, <u>o</u>, and <u>u</u>. Have your student tell you the short sound of each letter. Then have him tell you the long sound of each letter.

Review closed and open syllables. Build the word *met*. "Is this an open or closed syllable?" *Closed*.

Remove the <u>t</u>. "Is this an open or closed syllable?" *Open*.

Repeat with the words *bet, go, not, he, shell, she*.

New Teaching

Read "Off We Go!"

"Have you ever been sledding in the snow? If you didn't have a real sled, what do you think you could use to slide down a hill?" Discuss your student's ideas.

"Let's see what the children in this story do when they can't find a sled. Turn to page 143."

Have your student read the story "Off We Go!"

Read-Aloud Time Read a Story or Poem

Read aloud to your student for twenty minutes.

Track Your Progress

Mark the Progress Chart

Have your student mark the final star on the Progress Chart.

Celebrate!

Present Your Student with the Certificate of Achievement

3
Appendices

Scope and Sequence of Level 1

Your student will:	Lesson
Learn phonograms m, s, p, and a	1
Learn how to blend sounds into words	1
Learn about vowels and consonants	1
Read words with the sounds of m, s, p, and short a	1
Learn phonograms n, t, b, and j	2
Read more words with the sound of short a	2
Learn phonograms g, d, c, and consonant y	3
Learn that every word has a vowel	3
Learn sight word the and read more words with the sound of short a	3
Learn phonograms h, k, and r	4
Learn sight word a and read more words with the sound of short a	4
Read two short stories	5
Learn phonograms i, v, f, and z	6
Read words with the sound of short i	6
Read two short stories	7
Learn phonograms o, l, and w	8
Learn sight word of and read words with the sound of short o	8
Read two short stories	9
Learn phonogram u and the second sound of s	10
Read words with the sound of short u and the second sound of s	10
Read two short stories	11
Learn phonogram e	12
Read words with the sound of short e	12
Read two short stories	13
Learn phonograms qu and x	14
Read words with short vowel sounds	14
Read a short story	15
Learn phonogram th	16
Read words with consonant team th	16
Read a short story	17
Learn phonogram sh	18
Read words with consonant team sh	18
Read a short story	19
Learn phonogram ch	20
Read words with consonant team ch	20
Read a short story	21
Learn the sight word was and read words with consonant blends at the end	22
Read a short story	23
Learn the word to and read words with consonant blends at the beginning	24
Read a short story	25
Learn the words said and I and read words ending in ff, ll, and ss	26
Read four short stories	27-28
Learn the words for and no	29

Your student will:	Lesson
Read five short stories	30-32
Learn phonogram ck	33
Read words with consonant team ck	33
Read four short stories	34-35
Learn phonogram ng	36
Read words with consonant team ng	36
Read a short story	37
Learn phonogram nk	38
Read words with consonant team nk	38
Read a short story	39
Learn the word do and read compound words	40
Read a short story	41
Read plural words	42
Read two short stories	43
Learn additional sounds for phonograms a, i, and c	44
Learn additional sounds for phonograms o and g	45
Learn additional sounds for phonograms e, u, vowel y, and ch	46
Learn short vowel sounds	47
Learn to count syllables	47
Learn long vowel sounds	48
Learn open and closed syllable types	48
Read words with long vowels and open syllables	48
Read a short story	49

Appendix A: Scope and Sequence of Level 1

Phonograms Taught in Level 1

Phonograms are letters or letter combinations that represent a single sound. For example, the letter b represents the sound /b/, as in *bat*. The letter combination sh represents the sound /sh/, as in *ship*.

Card #	Phonogram	Sound	For the Teacher's Use Only (example of word containing the phonogram)				Lesson
1	m	/m/	moon				1
2	s	/s/–/z/	sun	has			1, 10
3	p	/p/	pig				1
4	a	/ă/–/ā/–/ah/	apple	acorn	water		1, 44
5	n	/n/	nest				2
6	t	/t/	tent				2
7	b	/b/	bat				2
8	j	/j/	jam				2
9	g	/g/–/j/	goose	gem			3, 45
10	d	/d/	deer				3
11	c	/k/–/s/	cow	city			3, 46
12	y	/y/–/ĭ/–/ī/–/ē/	yarn	gym	my	happy	3, 44
13	h	/h/	hat				4
14	k	/k/	kite				4
15	r	/r/	rake				4
16	i	/ĭ/–/ī/–/ē/	itchy	ivy	radio		6, 44
17	v	/v/	vase				6
18	f	/f/	fish				6
19	z	/z/	zipper				6
20	o	/ŏ/–/ō/–/o͞o/–/ŭ/	otter	open	to	oven	8, 45
21	l	/l/	leaf				8
22	w	/w/	wave				8
23	u	/ŭ/–/ū/–/o͞o/	udder	unit	put		10, 46
24	e	/ĕ/–/ē/	echo	even			12, 46
25	qu	/kw/	queen				14
26	x	/ks/	ax				14

Card #	Phonogram	Sound	For the Teacher's Use Only (example of word containing the phonogram)			Lesson
27	th	/th/–/t̶h̶/	three	then		16
28	sh	/sh/	ship			18
29	ch	/ch/–/k/–/sh/	child	school	chef	20, 46
30	ck	/k/	duck			33
31	ng	/ng/	king			36
32	nk	/ngk/	thank			38

Appendix B: Phonograms Taught in Level 1

Full Blending Procedure

1. Build the word with letter tiles.

2. Touch one letter at a time, and say the sound of each letter.

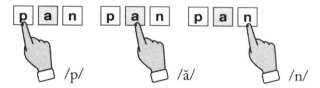

3. Go back to the beginning of the word and blend the first two sounds together.

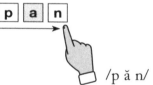

4. Start at the beginning of the word again. Slide your fingers under the letters and say the word slowly.

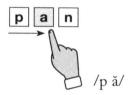

> **Tip!**
> Starting over at the beginning of the word is optional. Some students need the extra support provided by this step, while others do not.
>
> Whenever you feel that your student is ready, blend all three letters without this additional step.

5. Finally, say the word at a normal pace, as we do when we speak.

> **Tip!**
> **"Touch the Vowel" Technique**
> Many errors in sounding out words are related to the vowel. If your student says the wrong vowel sound, ask him to touch the vowel and say the vowel sound first. After he says the correct sound for the vowel, he should go back and sound out the word from the beginning.

APPENDIX D
Solving B-D Reversal Problems

Fortunately, most of the letters of the alphabet have unique shapes. No matter which way you turn them, the letter i looks quite different from the letter x, and f looks different from k.

There are two notorious troublemakers, though: the letters b and d. It is easy to see where the confusion comes in: flip the b and it becomes a d.

Beginning readers commonly confuse these letters. If your student is between the ages of three and seven, is just starting to read, and makes occasional reversal errors when reading, that is normal. It doesn't mean that your student has dyslexia or a reading disability. Make a gentle correction and move on.

But if your student is eight years or older, has had prior reading instruction, and is making frequent b-d reversal errors, it is important to take action to solve the reversal problem.

As reading instructors, we have two jobs to do regarding reversals:
1. Try to prevent confusion.
2. Where confusion exists, resolve it.

Job #1: Prevent Confusion

The first line of defense is to prevent confusion before it begins. The *All About Reading* program is carefully structured to minimize the likelihood of letter reversals. We teach the sounds of potentially confusing letters like b and d in separate lessons. The child's task is simplified because he only has to make one new visual discrimination at a time.

When your student is learning to print, be sure to teach correct letter formation. Doing so is critical to prevent confusion. When forming the letter b, start with the stick first, followed by the circle:

To write the letter d, start with the circle first, followed by the stick:

Have your student use lined paper so it is clear where the circle is in relation to the stick. Also be sure your student does not lift the pencil from the paper when writing any of these letters.

If you are working with older learners, though, it may be too late to prevent confusion. They may have had a few false starts in reading, and they may have already confused these troublemakers. They may encounter the letter b and misinterpret it as the letter d. They may read the word *bad* as *dab*, or *fad* as *fab*. You may give a gentle correction, pull out the corresponding Phonogram Cards, and re-teach the letters separately, but your student still mixes them up.

In this case, you need to move on to your second job as reading instructor:

Job #2: Resolve Confusion

The best way to clear up reversal problems is through multisensory teaching. Multisensory teaching involves multiple pathways to the brain: sight, sound, and touch.

Concentrate on just one letter per session. After that letter is completely mastered, you can add the second letter.

Teaching the letter b

Explain that the letter b is made up of a bat and a ball. When you are writing the letter, you first draw the bat part of the letter. Demonstrate this.

Have a variety of textile surfaces for your student to choose from. Possibilities include flannel fabric, corrugated cardboard, very fine sandpaper, fluffy fur fabric, or a carpet square. Ask him which surface reminds him of the letter b.

Then cut a large lowercase b out of the chosen tactile surface.

Demonstrate to your student how to trace the letter b on the tactile surface. As you are tracing, say "bat-ball-/b/," like this:

To further clarify which side of the letter the straight line is on, tell your student, "First you grab the bat, then you hit the ball."

Have your student practice this motion and chant many times over a two-minute time period. Repeat the exercise several times a day.

Show your student that when you are reading from left to right, you encounter the bat part of the letter first. If he is ever unsure of the sound this letter makes when he sees it, he should think to himself, "bat-ball-/b/." He will now be able to recall the sound of the letter b.

After the letter b has been mastered, move on to the letter d.

Teaching the letter d
Have your student choose a different textile fabric for the letter d. Cut a large lowercase d out of the chosen tactile surface. Use the new surface to trace the letter d, saying "doorknob-door-/d/." The doorknob represents the circle part of the letter, and the door represents the straight line, like this:

To clarify which side of the letter the straight line is on, tell your student, "First you grab the round doorknob, then you open the door."

Again, practice the motion and chant many times over a two-minute period. Repeat the exercise several times a day.

Show your student that when you are reading from left to right, you encounter the doorknob part of the letter first. If he is ever unsure of the sound this letter makes when he sees it, he should think to himself, "doorknob-door-/d/." He will now be able to recall the sound of the letter d.

After the letter d is mastered, do a mixed review of letters b and d. Continue to practice several times a day, and then gradually reduce the intervals between sessions.

Words Taught in Level 1
The number listed corresponds with the Lesson in which the word is first introduced.

– NOTES –

– NOTES –

– NOTES –

– NOTES –

– NOTES –